IN MEMORIAM HOWARD HANSON

The Future of
Musical Education
in America

The

The conference In Memoriam Howard Hanson: The Future of Musical Education in America took place July 5 through 8, 1983, at the University of Rochester's Eastman School of Music in Rochester, New York. The conference was co-sponsored by the Music Education Department of the Eastman School and the Music Educators National Conference. Published by Eastman School of Music Press, 26 Gibbs St., Rochester, N.Y. 14604, the proceedings of this conference are distributed through the Music Educators National Conference, 1902 Association Drive, Reston, Virginia 22091.

IN MEMORIAM HOWARD HANSON

The Future of
Musical Education
in America

Proceedings of the July 1983 Conference

Edited by Donald J. Shetler
Foreword by Robert Freeman

Eastman School of Music Press
Rochester, New York
1984

Library of Congress Cataloging in Publication Data

In Memoriam Howard Hanson: the Future of Musical Educa-
        tion in America (1983 : Eastman School of Music)
    In Memoriam Howard Hanson—the Future of Musical
Education in America.

        Held at the Eastman School of Music, Rochester, N.Y.,
July 5–8, 1983.
        Includes bibliographical references.
        Contents: Arts education and the arts endowment /
Frank S.M. Hodsoll -- The degradation of work and the
apotheosis of art / Christopher Lasch -- Music education
in the schools / Russell P. Getz -- [etc.]
        1. Music--Instruction and study--United States--
Congresses. I. Shetler, Donald J. II. Freeman, Robert.
III. Hanson, Howard, 1896–   . IV. Title.
V. Title: Future of musical education in America.
MT3.U5I48   1983   780'.7   84-3986
ISBN 0-9603186-1-5

Contents

Foreword

The conference "In Memoriam Howard Hanson: The Future of Musical Education in America" came at a timely moment in our history. Two months earlier the National Commission on Excellence in Education had issued its report "A Nation at Risk: The Imperative for Educational Reform," urging fundamental change in the fabric of our nation's primary, secondary, and collegiate education. Reforms concerning content, standards and expectations, and the commitment of additional time and fiscal resource are there put forward as vital to America's survival as a democracy and as an industrial power in the modern world.

Howard Hanson believed, with George Eastman and with those participating in this conference, that music in our new land can make a vital contribution to the future of America. Partly he saw this in terms of music's spiritual or aesthetic force. But partly he conceived this in a variety of other dimensions as well, for performance in a musical ensemble brings the participants together emotionally, working as a positive sociologic force toward collaboration in spheres apart from music. Certainly, music has a role to play in the development of community pride and in the useful absorption of American leisure time, a principal theme of George Eastman at the founding sixty-two years ago of the school that proudly bears his name.

During the course of this conference it was argued that musical perception is aural memory. If this is so, the development of musical education can play a powerful role toward the development of cognitive intelligence. Though it is often maintained that the educational reform which many believe will be given a high national priority during the balance of the eighties should concentrate on reading, writing, and computational skills, only a moment's reflection makes it clear that suasive speaking and writing are but the agents of clear thought and cogent analysis.

Musical education, properly conceived, has a great many vital roles to play in the future of our national life. I look forward to the counterpoint of our unfolding views. Howard Hanson's dream of a nation in which fine music is sought after by growing numbers of Americans is a theme to which all musicians and teachers of music will wish to dedicate themselves.

Robert Freeman

Director, Eastman School of Music
of the University of Rochester

Editor's Preface

"The Future of Musical Education in America" provided a forum for distinguished authorities to focus on critical issues facing all music educators today. Each contributed valuable insights into the aesthetic and social nature of man and emphasized the need to reassess current practices in music teaching and learning. This report of the proceedings documents the event, but even more important, it offers the reader a rich array of potential solutions to the broad range of problems the arts and education face in contemporary society.

This publication includes all of the addresses with virtually no editing. Summaries of group discussions that followed each presentation were prepared by graduate students in music education at the Eastman School of Music. Many hours of audiotapes were reviewed by Scott Prouty, Judy Bowman, Laurie Semmes, Craig Collison, Bill Grimes, Paul Stencel, Scott Shuler, and William Meckley. Summaries of the question periods following papers by Frank S. M. Hodsoll and Robert Freeman were prepared by the editor.

We are grateful to the Music Educators National Conference, John J. Mahlmann, executive director, and Russell P. Getz, president, for valuable help both in planning the symposium and assistance in the dissemination of this publication.

Without the diligent work of my colleagues in the Music Education Department—Roy Ernst, chairman, Milford Fargo, and Richard Grunow—the considerable task of planning and organizing the conference could not have been accomplished.

Robert Kraus, director of public relations for the Eastman School of Music, supervised the production of the publication. Phyllis Weltzer, Jan Grimes, Beverly Dartt, and Sharon Bennett contributed valuable assistance as typists and secretaries.

A final word of thanks is due Eastman School of Music Director Robert Freeman; his inspiration and enthusiasm for the project made it possible. Clearly, his leadership is in the tradition of the school's first director, Howard Hanson, whom we honor through the symposium and through the publication of this document.

Donald J. Shetler
Professor of Music Education
Eastman School of Music

Arts Education
and the Arts Endowment

FRANK S. M. HODSOLL

I am delighted to be here at the Eastman School of Music. Bob Freeman was good to invite me. It's an honor to be at your distinguished school, which has given so much talent and creative energy to the rest of the nation. This school has, as you know better than I, a national reputation for excellence in the training of musical artists and arts educators.

I am also pleased to be here under the auspices of the Music Educators National Conference. For seventy-six years, the Conference has encouraged more and better music education throughout the nation. We at the National Endowment for the Arts share your concern for continuing excellence in the creation and performance of fine music, and more broadly, for increased musical literacy for all Americans.

It is appropriate that you have organized this conference in the memory of Howard Hanson. He devoted his life to the field of music and music education. His forty years of service at the Eastman School gave impetus to both professional music training and general education in music. The world of music, and the world of Eastman, would not be the same had it not been for his leadership.

The scope of your conference agenda is impressive. I wish my schedule would permit me to be here when you hear from, among others, Sandy Boyd, who served with great distinction as a member of the National Council on the Arts, and Christopher Lasch, whose *The Culture of Narcissism* has earned so much comment over the past several years.

When Bob Freeman invited me to speak last fall, he in essence gave me a blank check while reminding me that music education was what this conference was all about. I would like to begin with a few words on professional music education and then turn to the general question of arts education of which music education is an essential part.

Professional Music Education

There can be no question about the importance of excellence in professional music training. Without the curricula and training opportunities provided by such schools as Eastman, Juilliard, Curtis, and many others, the nation would lack the quality of composers and performers which today makes this country a world leader in the field of music. A school cannot call artists into being; but it can and must provide potential artists the means and context for enhanced creativity.

Many of you will recall that in 1977 the Endowment established a Task Force on the Education, Training, and Development of Professional Artists and Arts Education. Chaired by Sandy Boyd and Martina Arroyo, the Task Force rendered its report in 1978, underscoring the need for greater emphasis on arts education—both professional training and general arts education.

It was in part as a result of this report that the Music Program in 1981 created its Professional Training category. We had given grants for this purpose since 1972, but the special category was not created until 1981. Only one other program—Theater—has such a program. The fact that the Music Program has this category underscores the priority attached to it by the field. We provided in FY 1983 $714,000 to assist thirty-six music schools to provide scholarships for aspiring musicians.

We are also particularly pleased that we are able this year to develop a partnership with the National Foundation for Advancement in the Arts to assist residencies for graduate student ensembles. One of the most urgent needs, in our perception, is the need to assist music students to bridge the gap between school and professional performance. It is our hope that this relatively small effort—which with matching should amount to $200,000 a year in FY 1983 and FY 1984—will help develop additional non-federal support for this purpose.

In addition, we would like to work with the music schools to develop realistic projections of jobs for musicians in relation to the supply of musicians. Our Music Program staff notes that placement of music students is difficult—partly as a result of too few opportunities, and partly as a result of many music students' inability adequately to present themselves for the jobs that exist.

The music field is similar to other performing arts fields in that too many students are seeking the "not-so-golden apple" of superstardom—making this "apple," as opposed to the process of becoming an excellent musician, their *raison d'être*. Hype is not excellence. We need in the schools to encourage excellence for its own sake—to provide a counterbalance to the societal tendency to replace heroes with celebrities. It was interesting to me that at our Dance Seminar at Jacob's Pillow last month, some of the most accomplished artists present there lamented the starry-eyed proclivities of younger generation dancers.

Arts Education

In considering the future, we must surely acknowledge the context in which that future may be constructed. In his current best-seller, *Megatrends*, author John Naisbitt approaches the question of past-present-future from a perspective somewhat different from that of Christopher Lasch.

Naisbitt concludes, among other things, that:

1. We have moved from being an industrial society to becoming an information society, implying that more than ever before our capacity to cope will depend in large measure on the quality of our education systems.

2. For the first time in our history as a nation, more than fifty percent of the adults in the country feel that they received a better education than that being offered to their children.

3. We have moved "from the myth of the melting pot to a celebration of cultural diversity." He also notes there are today more artists creating more works of art than ever before in our history. He talks in technocratic terms of "a Multi-Option Muse."

4. The action today is at local and state levels—governmentally and privately. This has, of course, always been true of education.

There are 15,600 local school districts and 3,152 private and public institutions of higher education. You, and your colleagues throughout the nation, work for and with the 97,000 local school board members. These school board members provide educational leadership and resources to 41 million elementary and secondary school students and 11.5 million students enrolled in 3,100 colleges and universities.

The *context* of arts education is complex and diverse. The *state* of arts education, notwithstanding some wonderful exceptions, can be summed up in one word—inadequate.

Schuyler Chapin, in his address two weeks ago to the American Symphony Orchestra League, noted André Watts's recent testimony to a Congressional committee that we are raising a generation of children to whom music is an elective, a frill. As our conservatories produce better and better musicians, our schools produce more and more ignorant audiences. Mr. Chapin correctly asked: Is this to be the mark of a civilized nation?

Laura Chapman, in her new book *Instant Art, Instant Culture*, notes that eighty percent of our nation's youth graduate from high school with little or no instruction in the arts. Few of the nation's high schools require study in any of the arts as a condition for graduation. And, few American universities and colleges require some degree of arts education as entrance requirements.

According to Chapman's studies, 100 percent of our high schools require no study of dance or theater for graduation; 98 percent require no music; 97 percent require no visual arts training; 95 percent require no English literature, and 94 percent of our high schools (a total of 25,000 high schools in all) require no American literature.

Therefore, and ironically, given the tremendous explosion of the arts both in terms of the growth in number of arts organizations and the growth in arts audiences, it is not surprising that the musical and artistic knowledge and sophistication of elementary and secondary school students across the country did not improve in the 1970s, despite the fact that youngsters were often favorably inclined toward both subjects.

The 1979 National Assessment of Educational Progress shows that in music, three-quarters of the students had positive feelings and were able to make simple judgments about music, though they knew less about music than their peers did in 1970–71. In the visual arts, museum visits have increased and students have demonstrated greater ability to create imaginative designs, but they were less tolerant of nonrepresentational art than in 1974–75, and their test performances on art have declined.

Several weeks ago the National Commission on Excellence in Education issued its report "A Nation at Risk: The Imperative for Education Reform." It contained a severe indictment of the state of our educational system. While this report was more illustrative of the problem than inventive of it, it focused much needed political attention on the matter. As David Broder has noted, education may well be, after the Economy and War and Peace, the major issue of the eighties. And, I would argue, we must make sure that the needs of arts education are a part of the debate.

The Arts Education Opportunities for the 1980s

It's always easier to describe problems than to solve them. But it is certainly clear that we in the arts must fight the good fight—not only for artists and arts organizations, but for the future health of our citizenry.

We do not start from zero. There are thousands of examples around the country (many of you may be involved) where exemplary and exciting arts education is made available to students. Universities, such as the University of Rochester and the Eastman School, continue as artistic oases of opportunity for students and educators.

Arts centers throughout the country—such as the Los Angeles Music Center—maintain highly active and effective arts education programs involving local school officials, teachers, community leaders, and, of course, students. But that center's president, Michael Newton, will tell you that, as effective as the program is, and as strongly supported as it is, it still reaches only about 180,000 out of a Los Angeles School District student population of 1.25 million. I should also note that arts institutions—such as the Boston Symphony, Atlanta Symphony, and Guthrie Theater—all have ongoing, effective outreach programs for young people in their regions.

In addition, a number of national organizations promoting arts education have emerged over the past several years. The Arts, Education, and American Panel report "Coming to Our Senses" has become one of the most respected public-policy documents issued on the subject; and the organization it spawned —Arts, Education, and Americans—has now merged with the Kennedy Center's Alliance for Arts Education, strengthening both organizations' capacities to impact public policy.

Organizations—such as your own Music Educators National Conference and the National Art Education Association and others—have spoken out often to promote greater emphasis on arts education and the allocation of resources for that purpose. The Rockefeller Brothers Fund, through its Arts Education Program, represents another strong leadership effort in this regard.

In addition to the efforts of the arts world, there are hundreds of schools with exemplary arts education programs. There are a great many teachers who feel strongly that arts education should be a part of the curriculum. And, there are many teachers—like the American history teacher who first got me interested in the arts in the middle fifties—who turn on, and open the eyes of, young people. The bottom line here is—has to be—good teachers who can communicate their knowledge and their feelings to the people they are charged with educating.

We in the arts world need to join the world of education, parents and students, in making the arts a basic part of education. What we are talking about is coalition building to implement what the Harris polls say is the overwhelming wish of most Americans—to have more and better arts education.

We at the Endowment recognize that the arts education issue is an enormous one. We do not propose utopian dreams, but rather marginal influences which may over time result in improvements.

We have begun, but not yet completed, our intellectual process in this area. What have so far emerged are four avenues for consideration:

1. We need to identify and assess education projects and processes that have worked and failed, and why. In this connection, we have just initiated a year-long study involving the New England states and New York to address a number of issues:

a) To survey, document, and evaluate arts programs in a specific region of the country,

b) To describe the public and private support systems which sustain these programs,

c) To develop a list of thoughtful "options" which identifies public policy issues, and suggests alternative roles for the National Endowment for the Arts and other agencies and institutions.

The study will be conducted by Tom Wolf of Cambridge, Massachusetts. Tom has been executive director of the New England Arts Foundation, and has taught music in elementary and secondary schools. He is also an accomplished flutist. He combines artistic capacity with educational credentials in that he has both master's and doctoral degrees from the Harvard Graduate School of Education.

Tom Wolf is well aware that he must include a wide variety of inputs in conducting his study if its conclusions are to be useful. He will work closely with the New England Regional Exchange Office, the association of the six New England state education agencies, and the Harvard Project Zero group.

2. We need to explore how teacher training in the arts can be improved. Clearly, improvement of American arts education will ultimately be dependent upon good teaching. And, the capacity of teachers in this area will, at a minimum, be assisted by their adequate training.

While I am not expert in this area, I draw counsel from my colleague Bill Bennett, chairman of the National Endowment for the Humanities, who has made improved training of secondary school teachers in the humanities a high priority. We will seek advice on this subject; but it seems to me that the question is appropriate.

3. We need to explore the use of mass communication, particularly television, as a technique of arts education. We have, in this respect, entered into discussions with the Humanities Endowment, the Getty Foundation, the Corporation for Public Broadcasting, Children's Theater Workshop, and the Department of Education.

We are considering the possibility of arts programming along the lines of "3-2-1 CONTACT" in the sciences. "3-2-1 CONTACT" reached millions of families. And, I am told it was followed by increases in school science offerings although the cause and effect relationship is not clear. The "3-2-1 CONTACT" programming included instructional materials usable by schools.

4. Finally, we need to assist the development of approaches which would bring more and better arts education to local school districts. As I have said on

other occasions, we need a campaign to translate the polls into reality.

At the same time, while I am convinced that there are thousands of concerned parents who would like to move in this direction, the choices are ultimately local and should be. Those of us in the arts can provide information and help, but the adequacy of arts education will ultimately be a function of the decisions of thousands of school boards. We must make them aware. We cannot, and should not, try to dictate.

Abraham Maslow, the late psychologist, had something to say about the value of arts education in his *Farther Reaches of Human Nature*. He wrote:

> Education is learning to grow, learning what to grow toward, learning what is good and bad, learning what to choose and not to choose. In this realm of intrinsic learning, intrinsic teaching, intrinsic education, I think the arts . . . are so close to our biological core, so close to this identity . . . that rather than think of these courses as a sort of whipped cream or luxury, they must become basic experiences in education . . .

The artist Yehudi Menuhin said it another way:

> The anatomy of art should ideally become the anatomy of our daily life, not in terms of isolated masterpieces but simply in terms of whatever we may be doing, moving from one place in the room to another, formulating our thoughts, cooking a meal, conversing. In the very art of living we should be engaged in artistic pursuit.

My distinguished predecessor, the late Nancy Hanks, spoke on this subject eleven years ago in Aspen, Colorado. She told a group of arts leaders and educational leaders:

> We have come to understand that we share common goals: We are all fighting *against* ugliness, against obsession with purely material things, against a sterile environment, against boredom. We are fighting *for* an appreciation of creativity, for we know the need for creative human action. We are seeking to enable individuals to develop a sense of purpose, a sense of wholeness and completeness, a sense of pride.

This is what we must work toward. We at the Endowment would welcome your help in the effort. Without it, we cannot succeed.

Question and Answer Session

QUESTION: Appropriations for the National Endowments are now in the Congress. How much do you expect to get for the arts endowment this year?

HODSOLL: The House Subcommittee has voted out a budget for fiscal '84 of $165 million. If we end up with a budget at that level I think that it will allow us to increase basic programs and to undertake some new initiatives.

As we went through a variety of budget levels and proposals, we tried to assess which ones could be implemented in the fiscal 1984 period, as opposed to fiscal 1985 where we also have new initiatives. In the case of fiscal '84, we hope to start a new initiative in the area of helping to enhance permanent theater companies. We will also be undertaking an increased effort in the area of touring—working through regional organizations and state arts agencies. Thirdly, we will try to increase the effort we started this year of encouraging a consortium of private organizations to help take out of the major metropolitan centers the more experimental and avant-garde work, so that it can be exposed to populations across the country.

In addition, we will spend a bit more on the Advancement program. As some of you may know, last year we put additional emphasis on our Challenge Grant program. If you look at the Endowment, we have our basic programs, which provide both operational and project support, and our institutional support programs, which are Challenge and Advancement.

We expanded the Advancement program to cover smaller institutions in all of the disciplines last year and the response has been so amazing in the areas of visual arts, literature, opera, musical theater, and electronic media that we would like to increase that substantially for the future so that we can help organizations develop.

I haven't mentioned education. The reason is that in terms of the four areas I mentioned today the big money—if it comes—is going to be in 1985. And we will be talking about the area of television as we prepare our 1985 budget.

We have set aside some significant monies for two or three of the items I have mentioned; one of them—the New England Study—is already funded.

QUESTION: You mentioned before that arts education is controlled by local school boards. We are sensitive to the fact that there are such uneven qualities among school districts. Education in other areas, those that are mandated, are the core of the curriculum. What's *left over* is what is valuable. Traditionally this has been a problem. Do you have a strategy to deal with that?

HODSOLL: I was speaking too loosely in confining my remarks to local school boards. Of course, state boards of education are a part of that puzzle.

From the point of view of the arts world, one would advocate at both the state and local levels [to make] the arts a more basic part of the curriculum—not subjects to cut first, as they traditionally have been. There is enough methodological analysis around to make the case that in addition to the "civilization" points I made in my talk, the arts contribute to other skills. Ultimately, given the nature of the constituencies involved, the best effort could be made with parents and PTA associations at the local level, the ones who are telling the national pollsters that they want more arts education. They have the votes to do that.

There is going to be a lot of national debate on the whole question of education over the next several years. It is very important that teachers and artists interested in education make their voices heard as curriculum review—teacher credential review and other things that are being mentioned—are discussed. It will require a lot of advocacy to see to it that it [arts education] doesn't get lost.

QUESTION: Do you see any new initiatives forging consortia between arts institutions, educational institutions, and business and industry, other than for the traditional endowment funding operation?

HODSOLL: I don't know the answer. Those who were promoting the "3-2-1 CONTACT" TV series, for six- to eleven-year-olds in science, had a great deal of difficulty attracting corporate support even for science. It's not clear to me why, but it ultimately ended by being a federally sponsored set of programs though the audience reviews were quite enormous.

In terms of arts education, we are talking to a number of corporations through the President's Committee. There are some prospects out there, but I don't know how significant they're going to be.

QUESTION: It used to be that arts educators would go to HEW or the Endowment. They would get shuttled back and forth. The Endowment would tell us, "That's not our responsibility. You have to go to HEW for that." Now that the program at HEW no longer exists, is it your intention that the Endowment will assume the responsibility as the only possible place in [federal] government that might do so? Beyond just another study of the problems of arts education—will you give us some money?

HODSOLL: I'm in no position to promise a lot of money. I don't think that the Arts Endowment would ever be in a position to become a major funder of arts education across the country.

Our basic mission is not in that area. Indeed, if you go back to the 1978 task force report, you will note that recommendations are primarily in the area of advocacy and helping to make connections. That is not to say that no money might be involved. I've already mentioned some money in areas like television, where I think that we can try to get other people to think as we do, to demonstrate the political process.

QUESTION: Might you stir the pot enough to get us back into the U. S. Department of Education?

HODSOLL: To the extent that the Department of Education maintains categorical programs—which are largely block grants to the states— yes, absolutely. I'm in contact with the top line in the Department of Education about that. Again, the department has chosen to devolve money out to the state level for redistribution. These are rather small categorical programs at this point.

QUESTION: I'm in the "parent" category. I live in Rochester and have been active with the Magnet School of the Arts here. I would appreciate some assistance in advocacy with our local school board. Does the Endowment have anything available—information or statistics—that we can use? I see increasing pressure from the computer literacy people, who are saying that all students *must* be computer literate. There is a lot more emphasis on math and science. I asked our superintendent what gets pushed over the edge when we increase graduation requirements in those areas. It's probably music and the arts. I didn't get a clear answer and I'd like to have some better tools.

HODSOLL: I don't have them yet, but that's what we're trying to develop. There are a number of pieces around. One that I would refer to you is the Educational Testing Service report, which includes several pages on the question of arts education and what it means to other subjects—how important it is in terms of educational testing. I agree with you that there is a lack of any central compendium of the kinds of techniques that will work. We've all heard about different approaches—and I'd be the last to say I'm an expert in this area. It is our hope that, starting with New England, we will go national in compiling these kinds of techniques and then work out a distribution system. I regret to say that it will take a couple of years to develop this source because the Arts Endowment hasn't done this before.

FREEMAN: To the people in western New York State, I would say that the members of the music education department of the school, along with other faculty and staff members, are always willing —on a volunteer basis—to try to twist people's arms in an advocacy role.

The Degradation of Work and the Apotheosis of Art

CHRISTOPHER LASCH

I accepted the invitation to address this distinguished gathering, I confess, in the hope that it would give me the chance to talk about a number of things I have decided opinions about: Beethoven's over-use of the diminished seventh; his addiction to chords in root position; the canard that Schumann couldn't orchestrate; the critical neglect of Ludwig Spohr; the Brahms-Wagner controversy (I believe the Wagnerites were dead wrong); the need for more compositions featuring prominent but easy parts for the viola. You will be happy to know that sober second thought has prevailed and that my opinions on these and other musical subjects—prejudices, I should probably call them—will remain private. They would not be of much interest to people whose ideas about music are much better informed than mine and backed up with years of professional training and practice (in the several senses of the word). Nor do you need to hear from me that music is the queen of the arts; that it combines the most immediate kind of sensuous pleasure with the most intellectual and abstract; that it provides the most compelling illustration of the possibility of disciplining feeling with form; that it uses the simplest and most economical means, an alphabet consisting of only twelve basic units, to achieve the most complex results; and that its capacity not merely to beguile the time but to order experience and evoke its depths is inexhaustible.

How music does all these things is a mystery I won't attempt to elucidate. I will content myself with a more prosaic question on which, as a student of American society and culture, I can hope to shed some light: how does it happen, in spite of all these riches, that the great tradition of Western music still remains so little understood and appreciated in this country? Why do the arts in general lead such a precarious existence in America? Why is the audience for good music still so limited, in spite of radio and records and all the other marvels of mass communication?

The fiscal crisis in education reminds us, in case we had forgotten during the boom years after World War II, that the fine arts still rank very low on the scale of American priorities. In the expansive educational climate of the fifties and sixties, the arts enjoyed a brief period of public favor; but the taxpayers' revolt, the shrinking tax base out of which education has to be supported, the end of the baby boom, and a series of deep cuts in federal spending have combined to force new economies on the schools; and in this climate of retrenchment, luxuries and frills are naturally the first to be dropped from the curriculum.

It doesn't do much good for friends of the arts to protest that arts are a necessity, not a frill. Such arguments are likely to make little impression on hard-pressed school boards hoping to rescue what they consider absolutely essential to the educational enterprise and confronted, moreover, with a powerful if misguided movement demanding a return to basics. Even a cursory consideration of the current plight of music education leads to the conclusion that the school system, especially in times when funds are scarce, reflects the state of American culture as a whole. The crisis of music education, as it has been called, forces us back to the question of why Americans continue to regard culture, with a capital C, as a rather dubious and peripheral undertaking, something not quite serious, something incidental to the more serious business of making a living and getting ahead in the world.

There is something a little misleading about this way of posing the question, as I will try to show later on. But first let me outline some of the answers that have been offered and explain what is wrong with them. The stock answer is that Americans are a young and still somewhat crude people, preoccupied until recently with the conquest of a vast wilderness and with the establishment of the material foundations on which a future civilization could hope to rise. According to this view of things, the pioneer spirit has lived on long after the work of pioneering was completed, carrying with it the cultural prejudices that art is not quite manly, that real men don't eat quiche, and that although a real man may go to the opera occasionally to please his wife, he won't enjoy it and shouldn't enjoy it and certainly shouldn't admit to enjoying it even if he does.

Another version of this explanation of American cultural backwardness stresses the commercial values long dominant in American society, themselves rooted in the pioneering ethic but endowed with the added prestige accorded in the twentieth century to business and everything connected with business. "The business of America is business," said Calvin Coolidge, and Charles Wilson, Eisenhower's Secretary of Defense, added that what's good for General Motors is good for the rest of the country. Such wisdom still summarizes an attitude that commands widespread, almost automatic agreement.

Another feature of American society that has allegedly inhibited the development of the arts is the country's cultural dependence on Europe, its cultural inferiority complex, its tendency to import culture instead of creating an indigenous culture of its own. The underdevelopment of American music seems to offer a particularly good example of this cultural colonialism. Until recently, our conductors and opera singers almost all came from Europe, American composers were held in very low esteem, and performing artists went to Europe for much of their training. Even today, the main tradition of Western music remains for the most part a European tradition. American music may now be good enough to be judged by the highest standards, but the standards themselves, it can be argued, are still set in Europe.

The cultural legacy of Puritanism has been singled out as another influence inhibiting the development of the fine arts in America. In the early years of this century, when American culture seemed to be on the verge of its coming-of-age, in the title of Van Wyck Brooks's famous manifesto, it was common to blame the underdevelopment of American culture on Puritanical repression and the Puritanical fear of beauty. According to Brooks, who developed the most sophisticated version of this argument, Puritanism represented the other side of pioneering, the spiritual equivalent of pioneering. Together they divided the American mind between them, the one "spectral and aloof," "sterile and inhuman," the other obsessed with practical results. Divided between two extremes, "bare facts and metaphysics, the machinery of self-preservation and the mystery of life," American culture had never developed the "genial middle ground of human tradition" on which a vigorous development of art and intellect depends.

A final line of explanation makes democracy itself the source of America's failure to develop a tradition of high culture. American culture is the culture of the common man, according to this view; it reflects a national commitment to social justice and to democratic standards of openness and sociability; and although it includes an admiration of art, it can't generate the kind of great art that is inherently elitist and anti-social, "resistant to gregariousness," and dependent, in George Steiner's words, on a "cultivation of solitude verging on the pathological."

In a recent essay, "The Archives of Eden" (*Salmagundi*, Autumn, 1980), Steiner maintains that the kind of culture that flourishes in the United States, in museums, concert halls, the record industry, the paperback book industry, is a "custodial," not a creative or original, culture. "Roger Sessions, Elliott Carter are composers of undoubted stature. Charles Ives is a most intriguing 'original.' Up to this point in its history, however, American music has been of an essentially provincial character. The great symphony of 'the new world' is by Dvořák." The weakness of American music, according to Steiner, is the weakness of American high culture as a whole. Rejecting the excuse that the country is still young, he attributes the meagerness of the American contribution to world culture to the preference, "thoroughly justifiable in itself," of "democratic endeavor over authoritarian caprice, of an open society over one of creative hermeticism and censorship, of a general dignity of mass status over the perpetuation of an elite" that is often "inhumane" in its conduct and outlook but remains essential to the production of original works of art.

The cultural price of democracy, Steiner argues, can be seen most clearly in the "disaster of pseudo-literacy and pseudo-numeracy in the American high school and in much of what passes for so-called 'higher education.'" Here Steiner's scorn for American culture overflows and finds its most appropriate object. "The pre-digested trivia, the prolix and pompous didacticism, the sheer dishonesty of presentation which characterize the curriculum, the teaching, the administrative politics of daily life in the high school, in the junior college, in the open-admission 'university' (how drastically America has devalued this proud term), constitute the fundamental scandal in American culture."

In one form or another, all these explanations of American cultural inferiority have been around for a long time, and all of them contain some part of the truth. Yet all of them misconceive the problem by exaggerating the degree to which the plight of high culture is a problem peculiar to the United States. In this respect, they are themselves symptoms of a national sense of cultural inferiority, which compares America unfavorably to Europe and ignores similar problems there. The crisis of high culture is not so much an American issue as a twentieth-century issue. The custodial attitude toward culture, the breakdown of the educational system, the attenuation of the creative spirit have now appeared in Europe as well, and not because Europe has been Americanized, as so many people complain, but because there is something intrinsic to industrial societies, I would argue, that is antagonistic to the fullest development of the artistic imagination.

If we look at the situation of contemporary music as a whole, what strikes us most forcibly is not the vitality of European music as compared to American music; what strikes us is the hostility of audiences to modern music, in Europe, just as in the United States; the self-conscious, self-referential, and academic quality of most of the music now being written; and the endless recycling of masterpieces composed in the eighteenth and nineteenth centuries. The musical tradition in Europe has become as custodial in its orientation as the American tradition. The passage of time has given the lie to the modernist dogma that great works of art find a popular audience in the fullness of time.

Except for the early works of Stravinsky and a few other isolated favorites, many of them written in earlier styles, the products of musical modernism have not established themselves in the symphonic repertory, and the recent attempt to revive the romantic style once again, precisely because it is such a self-conscious, often ironic undertaking, seems equally unlikely to generate a permanent body of acknowledged masterpieces. We have to face the possibility that the musical tradition in the West may have arrived, at least temporarily, at a dead end, and that the crisis of music education therefore derives, in the last analysis, from its attempt to disseminate a tradition that no longer has much life. If the Western musical tradition has become a dead language, then music teachers, like Latin teachers, will find themselves engaged in a rear-guard action, not to win a broader following for their subject, but to save it from academic extinction.

I said at the outset that the question of why Americans don't show more interest in great art or support it more generously is misleading. It is misleading in one respect because it treats as a purely American problem what is actually a Western problem; but it is also misleading because it exaggerates society's indifference to art. The decline in the quality of artistic production has taken place at the very same time that art has come to be taken more seriously than ever before. In modern society, art is not an object of indifference. In some quarters at least, it is an object of worship. It has come to enjoy the esteem formerly reserved for religion. Indeed the difficulty may be not that art isn't taken seriously but that it is taken more seriously than is good for it. It has been cut off from the rest of life and put on a pedestal. It has been relegated to the museum and to the concert hall (and the concert hall, as has often been pointed out, has become a museum in its own right) not because it is considered unimportant but because its adoration can best take place in an atmosphere uncontaminated by everyday concerns.

In earlier times, music often served as an accompaniment to other activities —dancing, socializing, religious worship. Only in the nineteenth century did music come to be segregated from ordinary life and surrounded with an aura of sanctity. This development coincided with the elevation of the performing artist, and above all the composer, to heroic status. Formerly composers had been regarded, like other musicians, as craftsmen, as members of the staff of educational or religious institutions, even as superior household servants. In the nineteenth century, the artistic genius for the first time came to be seen as a heroic rebel, iconoclast, and pathbreaker. (The cult of Wagner and of his "music of the future" played a central role in this glorification of the artist.) The flowering of music in the nineteenth century should not obscure the possibility that in the long run, this deification of artistic genius had very bad effects, leading to the dead-end of experimentation, the struggle for novelty and originality, the defiance of established forms and constraints, or their reimposition in the most stifling manner, that characterize the musical scene today.

It looks now as if nineteenth-century music represented the culmination of an earlier tradition rather than the dawn of a new golden age. It looks as if it owed at least part of its glory to a continuing dependence on its popular roots, to the persistence of dance forms and other reminders of the historic associations between music, popular recreation, and religious ritual. Nor is it a coincidence that it is the least pure of musical forms that have shown the most life in our own century: opera, ballet, even religious music, the continuing attraction of which, in an allegedly godless age, suggests that music is better off when the spirit of veneration is directed away from music itself towards a more suitable object.

The best starting point, for anyone who wants to understand the plight of modern music and the plight of the arts in general, is the book by the great Dutch historian Jan Huizinga, *Homo Ludens*. Huizinga traces the decline of the play-element in culture, as he calls it. "The great archetypal activities of human society are all permeated with play from the start," Huizinga argues. Language, myth, and ritual, but also "law and order, commerce and profit, craft and art, poetry, wisdom and science" are "rooted in the primaeval soil of play." Even those activities that are carried on with an instrumental end in view, Huizinga argues, have always contained an admixture of play, which enlists skill and intelligence, the utmost concentration of purpose, not in the service of utility but in the service of an arbitrary objective that has little importance in itself, compared with the arbitrary forms and conventions and rituals that define its pursuit.

The serious business of life, in other words, has always been colored by an attitude that is not serious in this sense and that finds more satisfaction in gratuitous difficulty than in the achievement of a given objective with a minimum of effort. The play-spirit, if you will, values the maximum of effort for minimal results. The futility of play, and nothing else, explains its appeal—its artificiality, the arbitrary obstacles it sets up for no other purpose than to challenge the players to surmount them, the absence of any utilitarian or uplifting object. But the appeal of play is so basic that it has always pervaded other activities as well, lending to religion, law, even to warfare an element of free fantasy without which they quickly degenerate into meaningless routine. And this is precisely what has happened in our time, according to Huizinga. The rationalization of warfare, politics, and work has banished the play-element from the workaday world and forced it to take refuge in sports, games, and art, which are collapsing under the increased weight now imposed on them. Art has "lost rather than gained in playfulness," Huizinga thought. It has become a "substitute for religion," and this "apotheosis of art," on the whole, has had pernicious effects. "It was a blessing for art to be largely unconscious of its high purpose and the beauty it creates. When art becomes self-conscious, that is, conscious of its own grace, it is apt to lose something of its eternal child-like innocence."

In many ways the most striking example of the historic process Huizinga was trying to analyze—the decline of the play-element in culture—is one he himself paid no attention to, the growing split between work and leisure. In most jobs, work long ago lost the qualities of playfulness and craftsmanship. Work no longer satisfies what John Dewey called the "unconquerable impulse towards experiences enjoyable in themselves." Today work is strictly a means to an end—profits for the capitalist, wages for the worker. The taste for beauty and the instinct of workmanship no longer find satisfaction in the work place and are therefore forced to seek other outlets. People who work at jobs deliberately divested of every challenge to ingenuity and imagination are encouraged instead to become consumers of beautiful objects, to cultivate an appreciation of great art and great music, to surround themselves with reproductions of great paintings and recordings of symphonic masterpieces. If they prefer the deadening drumbeat of rock and roll, this is not necessarily because serious music, so-called, is inherently unpopular but because it has become so closely identified not just with leisure but with the life-styles of the leisure class.

Great works of art have increasingly taken on the quality of collectors' items, valued because they advertise the wealth and leisure necessary for their consumption. The emergence of the elaborate institutions that preserve high culture today dates back, like the deification of art, to the nineteenth century. Opera houses, symphony orchestras, galleries, museums, the art market—these institutions monumentalized the wealth and social aspirations of the same industrial capitalists who were systematizing production, replacing skilled workers with machines, and redesigning the work place, in short, as an environment conceived strictly along utilitarian lines and deeply opposed to the spirit of play. Having banished art from the factory, the captains of industry proceeded to glorify it, and incidentally to display their own munificence and connoisseurship, in a setting carefully sealed off from popular intrusion, uncontaminated by association with the workaday world.

In industrial societies, art is doubly segregated from everyday life, in the first place because it retains so few of its earlier associations with ritual, sociability, and work, and in the second place because the glorification of art has gone hand in hand with its definition as a leisure-time activity and specifically as an activity of the leisure class. "Culture in America," as Thomas Hearn has recently observed, "is dangerously close to becoming strictly a class matter. If you drink beer, you belong to the union and watch television. If you drink champagne, you belong to the country club and go to the symphony."

The democratization of leisure has not democratized the consumption of high culture, and even if it had, the creation of a broader audience for the arts would not restore the connections between art and everyday life, on which the vitality of art depends. Works of art, as Dewey put it, "idealize qualities found in common experience." When they lose touch with common experience, they become hermetic and self-referential, obsessed with originality at the expense of communicability, increasingly indifferent to anything beyond the artist's private, subjective, and idiosyncratic perception of reality.

Those who love the arts and deplore their marginal status in American society need to rethink the task confronting them. The task is not to broaden the market for the fine arts, not to create larger numbers of enlightened consumers of culture, but to end the segregation of art and to achieve a new integration between art and everyday life. Instead of encouraging people to make better use of their leisure time, friends of the arts need to think about making the work place itself more joyous and playful, even if this means challenging the basic premises of our society. I don't mean that employers should be encouraged to introduce free concerts during coffee breaks. I have in mind something more fundamental: the restoration of craftsmanship, the revival of the artistic dimension of practical activity, the unification of work and play.

In a period of fiscal retrenchment, the question of justifying support for the arts assumes great urgency. Unfortunately the question tends to present itself to educators as a choice between a hard-headed appeal to practical arguments that practical men and women can allegedly understand and a more principled and dignified defense of art, on the other hand, based on appeals to its intrinsic value. The *Music Educators Journal* devoted its March issue to just such a controversy: "Utilitarian vs. Aesthetic Rationales for Arts Education." One side stressed the industrial, nationalistic, and therapeutic value of music. A proponent of the utilitarian position went so far as to argue that "music is one of the few remaining places in the curriculum in which a feeling of national pride is built up." Another utilitarian insisted that a discipline that "believes in its own lack of utility is doomed." The other side in this debate held that music is valuable, on the contrary, precisely because it resists assimilation to the "instrumental values" that are dominant in American society.

Instead of continuing this debate, educators might consider the possibility of reformulating the question. To formulate it as a choice between utilitarian and aesthetic defenses of music and art acquiesces in the divorce between art and practical life. This formulation accepts as the premise of debate the very condition that has led to the crisis of music and music education in the first place. Historically, the exaltation of art has been closely linked to the degradation of labor. Banished from the work place, the artistic impulse has taken refuge in the rarefied realm of art for art's sake. It is no wonder that the fine arts have lost popular favor; nor are they likely to recover it by a last-minute attempt to make themselves useful. The issue is not how to make art useful but how to make useful activities artistic.

This is not an issue, of course, that is likely to be settled in the schools. On the contrary, it will have to be settled in the work place. But the schools will play an important part in its resolution, if only because they have the responsibility of training the work force and can therefore contribute to a public debate about the kind of work force that is needed. A debate on this issue is already taking shape, and it provides an opportunity to reexamine the relations between education and industry, culture, and practical life. The educational system has come under intense criticism, much of it justified. A number of recent reports have linked educational failure to the decline of American productivity and the weakening of America's position in the world market.

The latest of these reports, issued by leaders of sixteen corporations and universities, including the presidents of Harvard, Radcliffe, Notre Dame, and the State University of New York, demands the integration of "domestic and foreign policies into aggressive, coordinated national strategies to meet the challenge of international competition." It calls for, among other things, a "displaced worker program modeled after the GI Bill," improvements in the training of high school mathematics and science teachers, "more competitive salaries for engineering faculties," and closer collaboration between industry and higher education in "problem-oriented research."

This is not a program likely to appeal to friends of the arts. But the debate over the connection between cultural decadence and economic decline creates the opportunity for those who reject this kind of program to offer a competing explanation of the crisis and a competing program for social and cultural renewal. They might point out, for example, that the schools are bad because our industrial system as presently constituted does not in fact need large numbers of skilled workers at all. As R. P. Blackmur once observed, it needs "only enough mind to create and tend the machines together with enough of the new illiteracy for other machines—those of our mass media—to exploit."

All the fashionable talk about the need to upgrade the work force through training in computer literacy, math, science, and engineering is based on a complete misreading of economic trends. The trend is toward a deskilled and degraded work force. The work force of the future will not consist of "information workers" and "data communicators." Skilled jobs will continue to be scarce. Already many industries that depend on skilled labor have exported production to places like Hong Kong and Taiwan, where skilled labor is cheap. Other industries are replacing skilled labor with capital. A careful student of employment patterns notes that the "major demand for workers in the next decade will not be for computer scientists and engineers but for janitors, nurses' aides, sales clerks, cashiers, nurses, fast food preparers, secretaries, truck drivers and kitchen helpers." The high-tech work force of the future is a myth.

Since music educators have nothing to gain from the rage for computer literacy and the whole high-tech program, they ought to be the first to challenge it. But the best way to challenge it is to call its basic premises into question, not to conduct a half-hearted defense of music as an adjunct to a technical curriculum. I don't see why music educators, and humanists in general, shouldn't be the first to point out that our society has little use for education in the arts, little use for education in general, because it provides most people with jobs that are repetitious, mechanical, and mindless. It gets the educational system it deserves; indeed, it probably gets a better educational system than it really needs in order to run the industrial machine. If Americans really believe in education, they had better think about changing the productive system so as to provide people with work that is challenging and artistic, work that really demands an education.

I don't think there is much hope for the arts and the humanities unless they become serious critics of the educational system as a whole and the society behind it. We humanists won't get much of a hearing if we merely try to defend our own turf or seek to operate as one more pressure group in a political environment dominated by much stronger pressure groups. But if we can join in a national debate on education as a whole and help to give a clearer focus to the widespread public dissatisfaction, not just with education but with the industrial system in general, we can make our presence felt. Instead of debating on our adversaries' ground, we can force them to debate on ours. We know more about the good life than they do. We stand for the things America claims to believe in but disregards in practice: truth, beauty, the full development of human capacities. It is time we made our voices heard.

Summary of Group Discussions

Group discussions following the speech by Christopher Lasch indicated common interests. Concerns regarding elitism in the arts were expressed by many participants. Reverence for the arts rather than active participation in them was discussed, as was the integral role of the artist in other cultures. One discussion leader noted the success of the "*Messiah* Sings" that seek to involve the general public, and suggested that expansion of this idea might spark increased public involvement in arts programs.

The concept of play as explored by Lasch interested several groups; most discussed the nature of play. Definitions preferred included play as fun, as goal satisfaction, as joy in achievement, and as involving imagination and creativity. Related ideas included play as purposeful rather than a non-goal-oriented activity, and the role of play in discovery learning. One participant, a college professor, questioned whether music education is really interested in the concept of play. Another cited the lack of a sense of play as evidenced by the absence of improvisation in school jazz performances.

A school music teacher expressed concern regarding orchestra players who are bored by the tedium of repetitious performances and students who will not play their instruments after high school because of disillusionment with the pressures of competition. Arthur Fiedler's approach to orchestral performance was cited as a positive step toward equating joy and music.

Computer-assisted instruction was discussed in several groups. A participant felt that teachers should use computers as an extension of the teacher, but that they should not be allowed to become the focal point of school programs. One group leader emphasized the effectiveness of computer-assisted instruction in infusing learning with a spirit of play, since well-designed computer-assisted instruction makes learning a game.

Several groups discussed the idea of music both as science and as art. It was noted that creativity, defined as new routes to productivity, is also possible in the sciences. The need to explore the uniqueness of music was noted, with a recommendation to reexamine classroom instruction. Many of the participants felt that aesthetic education should be part of all music instruction. The student as artist and "do-er" was mentioned; it was noted that performance classes provide opportunities to gain mastery and to share with others.

Several groups attempted to formulate summary statements. One participant stressed the responsibility of music educators to educate all, regardless of degree of talent or motivation. A group leader emphasized the persuasiveness of non-school influences, such as television, as well as the need to reexamine instruction with a view toward fostering the playful and the aesthetic.

Music Education in Tomorrow's Schools:
A Practical Approach

RUSSELL P. GETZ

The future has been clouded with predictions of nuclear confrontation and devastating events. This negative outlook has been detrimental to our national life style. It distorts every political action. It creates mental depression on an international scale. Those of us in education cannot be dominated by these fears or there will be no possibility of planning for the future.

We need to think in terms of gradual positive changes. Changes which we can guide and utilize to the advantage of the students committed to our care.

Over the past half-century music teachers have hopped on many bandwagons in order to justify the place of music in the schools. Ever since the Seven Cardinal Principles of the 1920s we have had to strive to convince educators, philosophers, and decision makers of the value of music in education. All of that effort seems to have made some impression.

The value of the performing arts in the school curriculum no longer needs to be explained or defended in the realms of educational planning and philosophy. Every recent report seems to agree that the study of music is vital to the development of an educated person.

The question today is whether music education has a serious and responsible program to offer, now that much seems to be expected from us. Are we really ready for an important place in the overall curriculum of the future?

Mortimer Adler, in his "Paideia Proposal" for the better education of all students, says that performance and composition of music will develop appreciation most directly and that aesthetic appreciation, the enjoyment and admiration of the arts for their excellence, is vital to enlargement of the understanding. "The best way to understand a piece of music is to sing or play it," he says, and, "All children should have such pleasurable experiences." "Of course," he says, "the Fine Arts are not useful or practical for most. If they were practical, they wouldn't be Fine!"

The Organization for the Essentials of Education, a coalition of some twenty professional educational organizations that has been combatting the simplistic Back to Basics dogma, in its statements of policy has included, among other things essential to education, the ability to express oneself through the arts and to understand the artistic expression of others.

The renowned College Board has recently included the arts as one of six areas of "basic learning." In its document "Project Equality: Preferred Patterns of College Preparation," the board suggests that skills for entrance to college include the ability to understand the use of the arts for self-expression by various cultures and to appreciate different styles and works from representative historical periods and cultures. It also recommends that students should have intense preparation in at least one of the arts and be able to express themselves in one or more of the arts.

The final report of the National Commission on Excellence in Education, titled "A Nation at Risk: The Imperative for Educational Reform," focused on what it termed the Five New Basics (English, mathematics, science, social studies, and computer science). Foreign language, fine and performing arts, and vocational education are complementary areas and "should demand the same level of performance as the Basics." Furthermore, it states, "a high level of shared education in these Basics, together with work in the fine and performing arts and foreign languages, constitutes the mind and spirit of our culture."

It is wonderful that arts education is now valued highly by the experts, but unfortunately most of their statements are not reaching the public. For example, when the Associated Press published its version of the Excellence in Education report, there was not a word included about fine arts. Letters calling attention to this discrepancy both to Associated Press and the *Washington Post* have been ignored. A condensed version by the San Francisco *Chronicle* actually states that fine arts are no longer included in the recommended curriculum.

This eighteen-member panel, appointed by Secretary of Education Bell at the request of the President of the United States, has had its report abbreviated and unbalanced. As far as arts education is concerned, it was eliminated by one swoop of a newspaperman's editing pencil. It is up to each of us to use whatever means at our disposal to explain to the public, especially school boards, administrators, and curriculum committees that are trying to comply with the new report, that the Commission does recognize the value of the arts and placed them very high in the curriculum.

One of the reasons I have organized networking systems within the Music Educators National Conference (MENC) is to train teachers and other volunteers with the proper communicative tools in order to speak out for public support of arts education wherever decisions are being made, and wherever there are wrongs to be righted.

Is there a conspiracy among the media against the arts or is it merely reflective of the ignorance of our average American citizen? *Time* magazine in its "Economy and Business" section of May 30, 1983, mentions the negative findings of the National Commission on Excellence in Education, and then has the gall to state: "High school curriculums have tilted toward home economics, music and driver education at the expense of the math and science needed for jobs in the new high-tech industries."

Music teachers have decried for years that the average high school involves only around fifteen percent of its students in any musical activities and we know that much of this is done outside of school hours. Yet, eighty percent of high school students drop science after tenth grade, according to the article. How jealous some critics are of the very small amount of time and personnel devoted to arts education, as if by eliminating the arts their educational problems would be solved. Shades of Admiral Rickover again!

So we, as musicians and educators, must continue the struggle for positive public opinion, unsupported by the press, without encouragement from a President who made his living in the arts, and in an environment where school officials are called on to push the basics, old and new, at the expense of those of us who try to minister for a few moments to the human spirit.

Having just returned from a short European tour, during which my choir was privileged to make music along with people from many countries, I am again impressed with the universality of music. We may argue the technicalities of whether or not music is an international language, but we cannot deny the roles it plays among all people, of whatever race or religion, of whatever place or time.

Wouldn't it be disastrous to one day wake up and realize that the rest of the world had discovered that the unifying cement which holds the key to peace and brotherhood for all people was their *love of expression through music* and the other arts, while in freedom-loving America this expression was stifled and ridiculed by a supposed highly educated and highly technical society?

In order for our citizens of the future to participate on a friendly basis with the rest of the world, our schools should be promoting the understanding of the languages and cultures of the world. In Austria I was asked by a native, "If a person who speaks three languages is called trilingual and one who speaks two languages is called bilingual, what do you call one who speaks only one language?" The answer: "An American."

In music education we must encourage a broader view by emphasizing the performance of both folk and composed music of our own and other countries. As professional educators we should ally ourselves with such groups as the International Society of Music Educators as well as with international choral and instrumental groups, lending them our expertise, but also learning through them of the incredible variety of musical literature, styles, performance media, and methodologies which are part of their various heritages and daily lives. Participation of our students in regional, national, and international festivals would be of life-shaping importance; sharing their music as well as getting to know more about other people.

What of the *quality* of music education in the future? One of our leading researchers, Ed Gordon, claims that music education is an infant profession in search of a discipline. This is a view that does not make him very popular with his peers, but it does point out that over the years music education has varied tremendously from singing for enjoyment and character building, to emphasizing sight-reading with solmization, to music for enjoyment and back again. Gordon's research demonstrates that the most important period for musical talent development is from birth to age nine. His tests, as well as those of others for the identification of musical ability, provide us with reliable means of discriminating between those who are talented in music and those who are not. This knowledge may then be used to individualize our instruction within the music classroom, analyzing the strengths and weaknesses of each child, and retesting periodically to measure the learning that has taken place.

This kind of careful teaching, with emphasis on singing, listening, moving, and creating, would greatly improve the potential of students K through third grade, thereby permitting all students to proceed far beyond present musical levels. Interestingly, the Excellence Commission also recommends that schools adopt rigorous, measurable standards and higher expectations.

A program of regular individualized testing further would demonstrate the quality of learning and teaching taking place, thereby adding to the academic respect for the discipline. It would also do away with the assumption that music is primarily in the affective domain and therefore not subject to measurement.

There are many other studies and reports that have emerged to help us develop better curricular standards. The 1982 Ann Arbor Symposium was a treasure chest of ideas and advice. For example, the paper on Task Involvement by John Nicholls of Purdue University could give new direction to present music teaching if its ideas were adopted. Just a few quotations: "When individuals are task involved, learning or performing is an end in itself. . . . Task involved people feel competent if they achieve their *personal best*. . . . When ego is involved, one's personal best or a gain in mastery is often not enough to produce a feeling of competence. . . . Ego involved individuals have to beat someone."

Of course, we need to learn to face competition. Competition can be fun, exciting, rewarding. The very selection of performers for ensembles is competitive, as is seating by chairs in band or orchestra. But building a program with constant emphasis on competition, whether by marching or dancing, singing or playing, is essentially ego-centered, built on the need to win by egocentric teachers, students, and parents. And in many of our schools competition has become the program!

This subject deserves the close scrutiny of musicians and educators as well as parents. Studies need to be made of the benefits as well as the disadvantages to students, schools, and communities of present systems of competition whereby groups of students are trained in minute detail on the execution of a very limited body of literature, sometimes with accompanying marching or choreography, so as to compete against other groups similarly trained.

What are the musical values to the student of the program based on winning? What are the financial costs, the expenditure of time of students, faculty, and parents for rehearsals, fund-raising and special events? And what are the long range aesthetic implications of using the art of music as a medium of competition, as if it were a series of barriers a group must hurdle? It may be essential to a professional's career to win a Tchaikovsky contest prize or for a barbershop quartet to be declared National Champions. Perhaps the contestants are mature enough to win graciously or lose without anguish. But what of the emotions and ill feelings associated with losers of all these school competitions? Music educators should be aware of all these consequences. The profession needs to take a position on the whole question of competition and make recommendations for certification of judges, educational values, and philosophy.

As professional music educators, we must have the courage to evaluate our efforts and to set out in new directions when the need appears.

One of the greatest changes for better music teaching was the gradual acceptance by general music teachers of the concept approach, as compared to previous efforts, which were often more concerned with associative properties of music. Instead of emphasizing story-telling through program music and correlating music with geography, social studies, mathematics, and science, the heart of music education has become the study of music itself, the components of pitch, duration, dynamics, and timbre, and the resultant concomitants such as melody, harmony, rhythm, instrumentation, style, and form. MENC identified Dr. Asahel Woodruff, among other leaders, as our patron saint of concept-based music education and somehow colleges, teachers, and publishers gradually joined the new flow. Not that we all use it perfectly—as Bennet Reimer has said, "there is no such thing as a botch-proof curriculum"—but the shift in emphasis has been a marked improvement.

If music education is to seriously accept the challenge of the future, I believe a new emphasis must be placed on what the College Board calls "intensive preparation." The implication is that music courses should require serious study and, as the Excellence in Education report suggests, "rigorous effort" and "the same level of performance as the Basics."

In order to accomplish this, MENC, along with other music organizations, needs to set new standards by which school officials, teachers, college admission directors, and parents can measure the quality and amount of music teaching the students are receiving. To be worthy of academic credit, music classes at the high school level should be comparable to the standards of the present Advanced Placement Program. Simply attending a general music class once a week has not successfully met these needs. In many cases both students and teachers have felt such classes to be unimportant and unworthy of their best effort.

General Music, or, as Roy Ernst has suggested, "Foundations of Music," classes, need to be better planned, designed for participation and learning. High school music courses need high standards of student expectancies and excellent teaching in order to be given academic credit. At the same time, if academic credit and proper recognition of the value of their place in the curriculum is to be forthcoming, performing groups are going to have to meet more demanding standards of a planned course of study. The old question of guidance counselors, "Why should Johnny be scheduled for band when he's already had band for five years?" must be answered with a program which can show, through proper evaluation, that annual progress is being made not only in terms of skill development, musicianship, and leadership, but also in the understanding and appreciation of the literature of composers of various historical periods and cultures. Such standards are not new; MENC has advocated them for many years. But given the present emphasis on entertainment, when school groups are utilized as public relations functionaries or low-priced substitutes for professional theater, and on competition, where the art of music is degraded to the level of inter-city rivalry like any sports event, such standards are in dire need of reexamination.

The most difficult challenge to change in this area will be in redirecting the efforts of many of our own music teachers into a music-centered, task-oriented philosophy, and to wean them away from the ego-centered attitudes that attracted many of them to music in the first place. Adding to the complexity of this change is the situation in which some of the supporting cast, consisting of school administrators, school boards, parents, and students, has been sold the idea by the music teachers that entertainment and competition are the heart and soul of the music program. So believing, they support it rabidly and expect it to continue. In our continuous struggle for parental support, we had better give them a *good* program to support.

Adding to the further consternation of any who attempt to change these attitudes is the business community, which has geared itself, naturally, to the public demand, using its advertising and salesmanship techniques to perpetuate the myths that entertainment and competition are worthy uses of school dollars and, if not tax dollars, then community dollars fund-raised by booster groups. These businesses vary from those which sell the necessary instruments, uniforms, music, flags, rifles, sound equipment, and lighting, to those which provide custom-tailored arrangements, coaching, adjudicating, and fund raising, to those who organize the contests, festivals, cavalcades, and competitions all over this country and abroad. It is a big business. It is Show Business. And why can't we just rejoice and be glad that all these people are very successful and having a good time, enjoying themselves and taking pride in their work, their kids, and their trophies!

The music education profession must set the standards of a comprehensive music program by which means administrators and parents can evaluate the musical value to students in terms of quality of literature performed, development of musicianship, demands on time, the effects of winning or losing at music, and all the objectives of a balanced curriculum.

In all of this, I am not trying to replace those traditional functions of entertainment, public relations, or competition, but, *through moderation*, to place them in secondary importance to our overriding cause, the development of each student to his musical potential, so he may better express himself and understand and appreciate the work of others of all historical periods and cultures. Music teachers should remember these goals as they plan judiciously to offer students a comprehensive experience. Administrators, parents, and the business community will be happy to support this approach to education. And the place of music in the overall curriculum will be strengthened.

Just a few words on the preparation of teachers. There exists in the various branches of the music profession altogether too much criticism of one another and too little respect for each other's work. While this is most obvious in performance situations, it seems to permeate our profession. In our universities, students are often caught in the crossfire between applied teachers and music education staff. When important issues are voted upon which may affect the preparation of music teachers, music education faculties have often been outvoted by a combination of the applied, theory, and history departments. In many cases the administrator is not experienced in education and thus fails to understand the significance of problems related to the school classroom.

A Ford Foundation study told us years ago that of those who graduate with music degrees of any kind, ninety-seven percent eventually teach! Yet many college faculty deny that they are themselves music educators, smugly setting aside that term for what they call "public school teachers." For years our higher education departments have used music education as a lesser alternative to degrees in performance, composition, or musicology, thus perpetuating the old saying, "If you can't perform you can teach. And if you can't teach you can teach teachers."

Unfortunately, these same professors who profess not to be educators do not attend Music Educators National Conference meetings, and do not see the enthusiasm and successes of our members. They avoid the public schools which provide them with both students and audiences, and are generally content to lecture or teach in the little ivory niche they have been able to carve for themselves within that well-known ivory tower.

These may seem harsh words, coming from a college professor, but I believe we can solve these misunderstandings and rid ourselves of the critical feelings. We *must* do this to save our program. And we need higher-education educators within the body of MENC to strengthen that organization.

Most of the dissatisfaction with music education, I believe, can be traced to our own education and to the dumping ground syndrome that colleges have permitted to develop regarding music education. That idea must be reversed. Isn't it logical that the best students be encouraged to enter music education, so that the vicious cycle of mediocrity in school music be stopped? Students of music should be screened for their love of music, their desire to share music with children, their ability to communicate and teach, for the musicianship, energy, personality, perseverance, and all those traits that are found in good teachers. These persons should be identified and encouraged to become certified to teach, while those who do not pass through that particular screen can still be encouraged to perform, create, theorize, historicize, merchandise, or organize music in any way they want.

How else can you build a profession that is worthy of the name? One more idea. Put a few of our best minds together and choose a unified undergraduate degree program for everyone. Take the very best portions of basic musicianship courses, the necessities of theory and history, the rigors of performance, add skill development on a member of each instrument family, as well as voice and keyboard. Since ninety-seven percent will teach anyway, give them all a dash of psychology and principles of teaching, so that when the day comes in which they teach they may do a better job. For those who pass through the screen, add some observation and student teaching, but for the rest—*everyone* will have passed (or failed) the same curriculum and therefore appreciate what the other guy had to do. No name calling, no accusations of watered-down or beefed-up courses of study—just the rigorous, musical training that will prepare students for the choices that must be made for career and future study. Then, at the graduate level, there will be plenty of opportunity to develop those individualized skills of performing, composing, researching, or teaching that are necessary for each chosen field.

I realize I have skipped over many of the practical developments of recent years and their future application to music teaching. I have said nothing of the right and left brain hemisphere study which has been touted by many to be our musical breakthrough opportunity. As further research goes on in this area, I sincerely look for more proof that the fine arts have a special function for the total education of the human being, in both mind and spirit.

I have said nothing of the various teaching methodologies in use today in our country, nor the adaptation of old or new means to make students more musically literate. This is not to say I am not interested or concerned. I am convinced that given the proper time on the school program we can—and, in fact, already are—teaching children to read music. Most of our instrumentalists can decode musical symbols and adapt them to their performance. It is only vocally that we have forsaken our responsibilities in many cases, but this fault should be, and can be, corrected once we believe it necessary. Only when the teacher is not convinced of the need for literacy, or is himself unsure of how to accomplish the task, does rote teaching prevail.

There have been gigantic strides made in the teaching aspects of both electronically synthesized music and the minicomputer. In my opinion, both sets of tools are of infinite value if correctly used.

The students who are early exposed to electronic music and who become familiar with music fundamentals through guided experimentation with sound generators, amplifiers, and modifiers are years ahead of my own generation. They ask questions of composition and timbre and form that didn't even occur to us at the same age. As for synthesizers replacing symphonies, as some have predicted, I think not. They already have begun to take their place as performing and compositional instruments. It will be up to us in the profession to keep abreast of developments and to use them for our curricular objectives.

Computers, mini and maxi, are also proving themselves as teaching devices, in addition to their splendid organizational potentials. Our lately departed friend, Buckminster Fuller, used to say that the school of the future might well be a student in his home with his own computer, bringing in by programming all the knowledge of the world, with no need for ever entering a school building. Somehow, when he told me that back in the mid-sixties, I pitied all those little chaps sitting in their bedrooms, with no need to put on their galoshes to go out in the rain, no yellow school bus, no classroom teacher to share her love and attention with them, no singing classes, no band practice. It did seem a remote idea as Bucky described it, and yet he lived to see the possibility come true.

I know we will utilize the computers to teach our children some of those facts, figures, and techniques they need to know, especially those aspects of musical literacy that are time consuming and seemingly so difficult to teach. But let us not forget the words of Rachel Carson in *The Sense of Wonder*, "If a child is to keep alive his inborn sense of wonder, he needs the companionship of at least one adult who can share it, rediscovering with him the joy, excitement, and mystery of the world we live in." Not the companionship of a computer, but a live, loving, humane music teacher to help him discover the beautiful world of music.

We are not ready for Orwell's *1984* in which the computers write the music and no one sings except the poor proles. We must remember to use all of the tools at our disposal, as *tools*, not as substitutes for the warmth and inspiration of the human teacher.

In summation, what I am calling for in our future is improvement in the preparation of music teachers, better understanding between all aspects of the music profession, the formulation of better standards of accomplishment throughout our school systems, more emphasis on early childhood talent development, and the acceptance of a task-oriented philosophy that has at its center the student, his ability to express himself musically, and to understand and appreciate the musical accomplishments of mankind throughout various societies and historical periods.

Our mission for the future is to collectively help our society toward achieving its human potential, that this country will have at last a vital musical culture and an enlightened musical public.

Summary of Group Discussions

The speech presented by Russell Getz stimulated discussion in several areas: the present status of music in our schools, teacher training, and the report of the National Commission on Excellence in Education.

General concern in several groups regarding the emphasis on performance groups in our school music programs, especially at the high school level, was expressed. At least two panelists stated that too much time was demanded of students with extra rehearsals and the like. Drilling and "animal training" can lead to dwindling interest on the part of proper musical readiness for performance.

Further, a good performance is not necessarily indicative of an overall healthy music education program. Too much priority on contests can lead to exploitation of students as well as student "burn out." Such comments in several groups led naturally to a concern about the welfare of general music students. How can we reach the general student population? We must enlighten the general public, and caution our non-music colleagues that performance isn't everything in music. This position could allow the development of substantial general music courses, especially at the high school level.

In relation to general music teaching, some participants cited the lack of a definite discipline in music as a major problem. Music educators go off in many different directions, and music teaching may, unfortunately, seem disorganized to administrators and non-music colleagues.

Several discussion groups dealt with music teacher preparation. Two opposing concerns were expressed in one group. Some criticized teachers who were not prepared well musically, while others said that most teachers are too specialized and narrowly trained. It was agreed that the earlier a student could get "hands on" experience, the better.

Positive characteristics that are essential for both in-service teachers and potential teachers were identified. They included enthusiasm for, and commitment to, music and music education, a love for working with children, ability to communicate, and a sincere desire for continued professional growth. One group also expressed the need for more attention to the role of the music administrator. Music administrative positions have too often been reduced to the role of "consultant" due to the narrow specialization of the music teachers supervised.

Lastly, most groups brought up the report of the National Commission on Excellence in Education with its many negative implications. There was general agreement that we must all be concerned with the report. As arts educators we must not let the "back to basics" cry allow further cuts in school arts programs.

The problems of cutbacks due to tight budgets and taxes were discussed. One group cited other problems hindering a musically educated society, including radio, cable television programs such as MTV, and the overwhelming power of commercial music industries in general. It seems that our young people are growing up with a need for great visual spectacles, even when listening to music.

We all must take concrete action in support of music education through political action, communication with the media, and becoming more active members of national support organizations.

The Phoenix Revisited:
An Etude in
Musicomythology

SYDNEY HODKINSON

We are all gathered here this morning at this present hour, to address the issue of our collective ability to influence the evolution of our country's future art education. Strong stuff. It is no mean task, for these are parlous times. While some of us may concur with columnist Carl Rowan's comment "If Johnny can't read, it might be because Ronnie can't reason," the recent (April 1983) horror report of the National Commission on Educational Excellence will certainly intensify the educational crisis. Perhaps this is fortunate.

The Arts and High Technology

The "Nation at Risk" reforms offered repeated endorsements of the fine arts, yet within our domain of *arts education*, all is not rosy. Recent writings on the "New Liberal Arts," born out of a sense of inadequacy between science and the humanities, highlight this new Sputnik Age. Calls for applying math/science training to routine problem-solving, understanding technological matters, feeling at home with the computer, are now heard everywhere. The strongly growing feelings in our country with technological literacy now exemplified by, for example:

1. 29,000 schools possessing microcomputers (an eighty percent increase in elementary schools over the preceding year),

2. the creation of new high schools devoted only to science, math, and engineering,

3. rampant curricular changes in many universities,

4. the House of Representatives passing a $425 million bill to improve the training of science teachers,

5. even second-grade students learning to program three-foot robots.
—all of these conditions result from concerns that are honest and heartfelt.

As was eloquently pointed out by Mr. Lasch, the now-playless business of Business will have a profound effect on our culture generally and on arts education specifically. The current anxieties will alter us all.

Many of us never felt comfortable with "science" in the first place and are even less sanguine about today's High Technology; much must be done to seek an enduring balance.

The comment from a Massachusetts subscriber to the *Music Educators Journal* following its January 1983 issue on new technology—"I think . . . [it] is a complete disgrace. The editors should be hung for treason along with their computers!"—is, I think, an opinion echoed by thousands of educators. The "New Liberal Arts" will not be warmly espoused by those who earned a Master or Doctorate of Education degree without even going near the Xerox machine.

Although it has been said that the only deadly sin is cynicism, please know that it is often very difficult for a composer to look at arts education—and certainly its future—without feeling like the Milan Kundera hero who walks into the town square, sees an old man vomiting grotesquely in a corner, ambles over, places his hand on the man's shoulder and says: "I know *just* what you mean." However, I do concur that cynicism is poor medicine, and wish to offer a few personal thoughts on the present state of music education, our contemporary media, new music and performance today, and to offer proposals for the future, all in the most positive and hopeful spirit.

While my own experience as a hands-on secondary school teacher ended over a quarter-century ago, I have never allowed my ignorance of a subject, as some sage once remarked, to keep me from sounding-off about it.

The Phoenix Arising

Personal lectures in the past oblige me to confess that I agreed to Robert Freeman's invitation—to offer an artist's viewpoint—with great trepidation. Over lunch recently, a leading American music publisher told me that he did not speak to music educators any more because it just didn't seem to do any damn good. From my own meager attempts in this regard, I can only report that offering any advice to others often resembles a professional wrestling match; the grunts, groans, slaps, and shrieks resound briefly throughout the land, but no permanent injury seems to result.

Still, we are here this morning, not unlike the Phoenix awaiting rebirth, committed to the future life of our organization and believing that "the long habit of living," as Thomas Browne said, "indisposeth us to dying." And dying —like the Phoenix after the triumphant years—is what will surely follow without something more than Band-Aid applications/Money Hunts and indeed—like this week's activity—*talk*.

The Phoenix comes the closest of all the mythological beasties to being a conventional animal, all "Bird." At a casual glance, the mythical animals seem exotic nonsense, totally obsolete. So we say. The Chimera, for instance: a fire-breathing monster with lion's head, goat's body, and serpent's tail; the Manticore, an oriental beast with parts of scorpion, lion, and man; or the Centaurs, Griffins, and all the rest are like bad dreams to be discarded. So we say. They are, in fact, like dreams—and not necessarily bad ones. In truth, however, we may have a hard time doing without them. These bestiaries do not, as a rule, possess totally imagined features, but are made up of parts that are entirely familiar to us. What is novel is that they are *mixtures of species*.

It is precisely this amalgam of kinds that, in part, I wish to speak with you about. Our work involves many aspects and the future of our labors must involve that mixing of species. We must create our own Phoenix in order to preserve the initial objectives of the MENC Constitution.

The Goal/Objective Dissolution

The 1970 GO (Goals and Objectives) Project, with true Phoenix-Reborn-idealism, stated "MENC shall conduct programs . . . to build a vital musical culture [and] an enlightened musical public." MENC will develop "exemplary models of desirable . . . practices in music teaching . . . and programs of study that correlate performing, creating and listening . . . encompass[ing] a diversity of musical behaviors." Strong stuff. The Project also said that these goals "constitute . . . a basis for action . . . calling for continual reexamination . . . to evaluate the effectiveness of its policies." *Let's!*

Are there many here this morning who truly feel that the idealistic MENC-"Phoenix"-concepts are efficaciously carried out nationally? What has changed? What happened to the initial dream? For one thing, a large base of educators has simply failed to keep up with the aesthetic changes of the artists. While recent trends have now allowed more "wobble-space" for non-Western, folk, jazz, and pop musics in the classroom, the European-Meisterwerke-WASP-output still commands much of our attention. The American artistic community, initially a relatively small group in the twenties and thirties, has now profoundly grown, altered, and inexorably *improved*. But we fly on—also inexorably—a blind Phoenix largely doing the same things in the same old ways, asking the same tired questions, often applying the same passé "techniques"—all to entirely different conditions. The goals and ideals remain the same, but these objectives are all too often being applied to an artistic society that is dramatically different. One is in trouble if one observes the apple rolling uphill and still believes in gravity. Yet, the failure of most educators to adapt to any new tide not only elicits pity, but it becomes positively debilitating for our trade.

I'm well aware, as are you, that ignorant people are to be found just as often among the educated as among the uneducated, but the lack of adaptability—alas, even among some of our younger teachers—is, in my experience, inexcusable; it supplants the natural inquisitiveness of the young with the prejudices and set practices of the "old-pro" teacher.

Nowhere does the inability to change any of our thinking more manifest itself than in many teachers' lack of rapprochement with contemporary creative thought. (I will return to this point later.) Although we now have hundreds (probably thousands!) of fine school bands, orchestras, and choruses in our land, are their members allowed any *real* insights into the workings of the creative imagination? Is there generally a more benign acceptance, or more even-handed toleration, of the works of today's composers? Are all students truly allowed exposure, in the words of the MENC objectives, to "music of *all* periods, styles, forms, and cultures"? As a result of our past arduous labors, are the present heads of our national symphony orchestra boards—often our past music students—more open-minded or genuinely interested in an expanding repertoire? Or is it just Business-As-Usual: Opera plus the Big Name equals culture, or Tchaikovsky's Fourth and the *Eroica* every season?

Neither, as a result of our "effort to *examine* the present and project into the *future*" (MENC's terms), have there developed any intact philosophies defining satisfactory public service. Nor are we alone. Television executives, often explaining that real public service is shown by anything in which a large portion of the audience is interested, would therefore have us believe that even "Hee-Haw" and "Family Feud" are in the public interest. In our educational field, we are fortunate that decent arrangers can offer young students more-or-less "real" Mozart, Haydn, and Beethoven transcriptions, for example. But to play *ad nauseum*, as many do, only C&W Hits/rehashed Debussy, "educational music," rock charts foisted upon us continually by publishers trying to stay afloat—to do this all because it is "of interest" to the students under our charge is to invite sure-fire aesthetic disaster. I feel we are on the verge of allowing the machine to run away with itself instead of keeping pace with the educational needs it was created to serve. Further, let us make things better before the students stop coming to us.

Can we not keep safe some of their creative gray cells from such a deluge of trivial banality? Why fritter away the minds of the young? It is our most precious national resource, capable of totally rekindling our Phoenix-Ashes. Still, even in very high-quality school organizations, ninety percent of what I hear played is a perverted, bland, long-range "fallout" from music, the result of a comic-book mentality, that we will pay for dearly in the future; later generations will hold us accountable.

The search for blame abounds, of course, and it's not, we may all take comfort in knowing, all our fault. I will return later to the special problems of new music and education, but for now, let us continue our Phoenix-Flight to where I've obviously been leading you, to the Largest Nest of All: today's media.

The Media

The American poet Archibald MacLeish leaves no doubt about his attitude on the importance of broadcasting: ". . . (it) matters far more over the long run . . . than what anybody else does because (it is) more persistently shaping the minds of more people than all of us put together."

Strong stuff.

The media determine, as they will in the future, what kind of people we are. It's a sobering thought; for how many of you here this morning wish to have our society, or your part in it, remembered by "Three's Company" or "Tic Tac Dough"? (Tit, Jiggle, and Greed.) But I do not intend, you'll be pleased to know, to denigrate that "vast wasteland." Others associated with the media business have done so far better than I could ever hope to. If video tapes of the three major networks' products could be preserved, future historians would there find recorded, as Edward R. Murrow declared twenty-five years ago: "evidence of decadence, escapism, and insulation from the realities of the world." "History will take its revenge, and retribution will (catch) up with us." Perhaps, for us musicians, it is here now.

The current status of our media and its appalling relation to serious art is known to you all:

1. on radio/television: just turn on your sets . . .
2. in the print media: never underestimate it.

A composer at Eastman, recently showing me a 144(!)-page monograph on the Punk Rock group "Plasmatics" (144 glossy print pages with full-color pictures), strongly reaffirmed my belief that the music talked about is the music that is played; the music written about is the music recorded; the music that is widely disseminated is the music people listen to.

3. on recordings: Is one ever made aware of any classical music in a record store? The strong implication is not only that the rock and pop merchandise is all that is available, but that it is the only type worth buying.

First-class music education, it seems to me, has not escaped a similar fate. While, in its infancy, it was supposed to be "enlightening, vital, exemplary, and diverse" (MENC's terms), it is now tending to become the creature, the servant —indeed, the whore—of "General Merchandising," all too often like the media-hyped cars, refrigerators, and clothes we buy, the sports/entertainment with which we are inundated, and the books/papers we are admonished to read. Large sales of television and sci-fi movie "themes," ineptly written rock arrangements of the Tunes of The Stars—a bubble-gum Top 40, in short—these offerings gobbled up by music educators keep many of our prestigious publishing houses in business. There is a place for such material, I do not deny it. But I question it a) as totally *dominating* fare, and, b) coming at a time when an artistically enlightened populace may mean the difference between the survival of our trade or its erosion. Such courses of action simply replace their own rendition of "decadence, escapism, and insulation" for any honest clarification or interpretation of the best of our sonic art. To turn a movie theater into a burlesque house, a nature-food store into a porno shop, is the owner's prerogative. But, to so transform a school's rehearsal rooms or university teacher-training curricula—both set out to EDUCATE—is surely something no civilized person would tolerate.

If those music teachers and, no less, symphony orchestra boards continue to pander by giving the public what it wants to hear, instead of reserving some space in order to offer what knowledgeable directors believe people would like if only they had an opportunity to know about, then their initially instigated charters as cultural forces in our society are entirely negated.

Today, education often does as much to thwart any recognition of real individual imaginative experience as the lack of education limits same. Amid the two extremes of the "Art-Only" enthusiasts on one side and the "Entertainment/Populist" advocates on the other, some secure place has to be found. It must be done for the simple reason that one does one's best because it's the right thing to do. So many of us today in music education are overly discouraged owing to the many problems of budget, space, and community support, often resulting in a denigration of ourselves and our job in society. Russell Getz, the president of MENC, said it so beautifully and simply: "If you do *good* work, [citizens] will appreciate it and respect you for it."

If I presumed earlier to broaden the base of a thesis on what is, for me, the unfamiliar landscape of technology, arts education doctrine, today's media—even elementary mythology—I now wish to enter for a few moments into my own element: music and the composition thereof.

Alas, not all of the mythical beasties I have mentioned are friendly, although even the most hostile among them have certain redeeming, amiable aspects. Let us briefly consider today's composer and the ramifications of his work *vis-à-vis*: 1) the audience, 2) educational research, 3) the classrooms, and 4) performance practices.

The Composer and the Audience

Edgar Varèse's statement, that he would not earn enough money from his music to pay for his own funeral, is an apt summation of the plight of today's classical creative artist. It is a sad thing for a composer to admit, especially while spending so much time producing art, that our music is probably not going to survive at all. We have no audience. Notwithstanding the current "a la mode" minimalist school turning people away in our larger cities, the audience for new music, as I've stated repetitiously before in detail, consists of barely the Hardy Few.*

For teachers, the "performing art only" and "public acceptance" syndromes rear their heads continually in our work. Educators who equate a mass audience's acceptance as a measure of the worth of an artist's work entirely misconstrue the very function of educational institutions. Schools, from kindergarten through the postdoctorate levels, have a duty to help students understand the arts, not just practice them. Furthermore, in music, unlike sculpting, writing, and visual arts classes, our practice of performance—re-creating, not creating—does not enhance comprehension of the imagination one whit! Music educators who also compose have an important part to play in aiding such understanding, not only by what they teach and their manner of doing so, but by their presence as role models. (I'm still absolutely amazed—even last year, in a grade six classroom in Penfield, New York—by how many children still think of all "classical" composers as being old, white, bewigged, and undeniably *dead*.)

All the bromides about the lack of audience communication fail to confront the questions: Which audience? The bravo-opera audience? The evening subscription series? The Baroque chamber music audience? If size of auditors is so impressive to us, do you not recall that the largest audience of all (e.g., those 300,000-plus Rock fans in California last May) right now regards Mozart as a "geek," Bach as "grody to the max" and Brahms as strictly TTFW ("too tacky for words") unless their music is backed up by "cool" synthesizers and a Fender bass? Three weeks ago, in a Pennsylvania restaurant, the Moozak for this audience offered the latest effrontery: a discobeat bastardization of Grieg-Liszt-Beethoven-Mendelssohn-Bizet and on and on—eight bars of each, switching from one to the other, for over three minutes! Of course, we are all insulted by such debauchery. Does anyone here suggest that today's classical composer write to satisfy this audience??

People—our past students—have simply not been trained to absorb most twentieth-century music nor, indeed, have they been living in a cultural utopia that nurtures such training. We often forget that a large percentage of Brahms's

---

* "The New Music Ensemble in the University," *College Music Symposium*, Vol. 18, No. 1, Spring 1978, pp. 109–119.

audience, for example, played and read music, even around the home, having none of our present media to pacify them. Today, folks read James Bond novels while listening to records! I once knew a man—a college music educator and administrator, *honestly*—who, at mealtime, stacked all the Beethoven quartets on his record player and played them through two movements at a time so as not to disturb his dinner!! In our time, we have individuals managing arts councils, voting on boards of symphony orchestras, acting as the leaders-of-culture in our communities, who have never seriously concentrated on any one piece of music in their whole lives. And they were very often *our* former students!

We've got our just desserts. And make no mistake, these people are not only the older denizens of a country that we were going to make musically "vital" and "enlightened." Our culture has never allowed a tradition of serious music to intrude upon it. The sheltered comfort provided by the average lay concert-goers' comment that, "if I don't know the piece, then it's not worth knowing," provides *zero* solace to a music teacher, surely.

The Composer and Educational Research

I respect, and often greatly admire, the work of scholars and philosophers who patiently distend and perfect their knowledge of a specific topic the way musicologists zero in on particular centuries or nations.

I think, however, that such endeavors should be made more accountable to matters of general artistic and comparative creative scope. The inability of many research experts to a) do combat with the aural salad bowl of new music, or b) attempt coherent discussion about the *causes* of current predicaments of art training, is probably owing to the very fact that we confer admirable prizes—a communal bonus—on specialists who only infrequently endanger a fact with any hypothesis. It seems to me that the proportional relationship between the *volumes* of music education research and the *depth* of educational confusion speaks for itself.

This state of bewilderment is due to a shortage of studies, cry the research pundits. If these scholars have their way, we shall, I fear, know *less*, not more. For without trying to bridge, to link up the peculiarities of the imagination with the artistic brain, without logically arranging our already extant wisdom regarding efficacious instructions—in short, to attempt to explain Joseph Haydn's *head*—more "research" will only do us in! If we genuinely seek a clarification of our objectives, we must at least have a rough idea about where to start looking; and, as a starting place, I suggest the possibility of today's music classrooms.

The Composer and Today's Classroom

The attempts over fifteen years ago by the Canadian composer Murray Schafer, in his school booklets, were all designed to do one thing, what John Cage also advised: LISTEN! This "ear-cleaning" educational music, including pieces by, for example, Schuller, Rhodes, George Self, Rorem, Smalley, Erb, and many others (including myself), and the pioneering work of Carl Orff, is still almost totally ignored by large segments of the music education community.

The critical problems of opening up the ears of youngsters from five to twenty-five, say, are not at all solved—believe it—by the following examples I have observed within just the past five years:

1. The junior high teacher, in the middle of the first movement of a Mozart G minor recording, banging on her desk to try to becalm an unruly class and shouting: "Quiet! Listen to this!! It's a *MASTERPIECE*!!"

2. The elementary school choral director reciting to her charges that the melodic tritone was "an unnatural interval, and impossible to sing."

3. The state university music appreciation instructor allotting his semester's last three classes for "Music since World War II."

4. The district music supervisor stating that he had to spend so much time disciplining "errant" teachers, codifying schedules, and attending committee meetings that he could not afford time to either investigate classroom music instruction or even think about methods to lead his responsible teachers into finding ways to offer aesthetic, creative training to the children of his district.

5. The high school band director erroneously offering a musical education to his students by: a) playing 1950s musical comedy tunes for the Rotary Club luncheon, b) evolving new marching formations for the gridiron, c) performing an entire spring concert consisting of commercial rock charts because "the kids really love 'em," or d) going on a tour to the Bahamas for what is euphemistically termed an "international music festival."

Enough, enough. I hear your groans. It is possible—indeed, quite likely—that all of you here (especially since you took the time to come to this summer conference) know of these things and know them to be true. I only recall them to make them active to you again, not to denigrate our jobs, just as I would like you to recall them to *me*.

Concern for the quality of educational music is commonly rebutted by such questions as: "What *is* the best and the worst? *Who* determines what music is good and what is bad?" May I offer a tiny experiment, not altogether facetiously? Could we attempt to form a small, closed-room jury of our country's leading educators, school conductors, and administrators, and compel them to listen, just for a single day, from 8:00 a.m. to midnight, to all of the "educational" music published by the American houses during the past six months? Perhaps we might even videotape their reactions! I feel certain that the judges' own pride, artistic knowledge, and overall good judgment would quickly offer us a sense of what is good, what ill.

The composer, the publisher, the educator—all of them—are not blameless for the current paucity of superb educational music. I have spoken before about this triumvirate* and will not "chew my cabbage twice." It is indeed a Witches' Dance of primaeval force in our musical life, capable of stomping beneath its collective steps even the most hardy and noble Phoenix Nest. Allow me one small

---

* "Ramblings from a Composer's Desk," *NSOA Bulletin*, Jan./Apr. 1976; "Concerns from a Composer's Desk," *The Instrumentalist*, No. 32, Sept. 1977, pp. 93–96.

"cabbage-chaw" as a most gentle reminder, however: Just because a composer writes something that you do not understand, or even like, does not mean, *ipso facto*, that he is an uncommunicative, incompetent ass. The music classroom quandary leads ever onward to unfortunate results when one considers the plight of performance.

The Composer and School Performance Practices

I have documented earlier,* for the College Music Society, my personal thoughts about the role of music performance in our educational institutions. Some performance before an audience is mandatory, but how much? How much longer do we continue to turn out excellent re-creative practitioners—the first-class "fingerers"—without paying at least equal class-time dues to the creative and aesthetic understanding necessary to assist, further along in time, our professional art organizations? Men and women, now in their forties and fifties who were taught music education in past years by you and me, are now sitting on the boards of American symphony orchestras *firing* conductors because the latter are performing too much of "all that new stuff," and, like as not, hiring the wavy-haired European to play the *Emperor Concerto* yet again.

The tenacious, omnipresent emphasis on performance in our schools is another species of Bird, and one that soars over all. However, this one is dark, foreboding, and more resembles a pterodactyl or a plastic-something from the Star Wars trilogy. It produces in its shadow large numbers of children who can finger perfectly an E-flat major scale, yet do not know how Mozart or Dvořák ever put it to use. It yields gifted high school students who can play *The Rite of Spring* (in a band arrangement, no less), yet do not have the faintest glimmerings of the type of cohesion or rhythmic intellect that Stravinsky poured out, much less any wisdom as to the influence of this work on myriads of younger artists. This bird manufactures, even in our leading universities and conservatories, hundreds of students—in a constant stream—practicing their Puccini/"Pathetiques"/and Paganinis, all of them majoring in Anachronism 101.

These are inflationary times. And nowhere is the consummation of cultural inflation more rapacious than in the glutted Music-Stardom-Lottery. The conventional musical fare is patently unable to support more than a mere handful of top-flight performing artists. Yet, in that steady river of new contenders afflicted with Perlmanitis, we are coming close to Andy Warhol's prediction that, in a few years, we'll all have been famous for about fifteen minutes. My own decade-long association with Eastman students reaffirms my opinion that players are beginning to realize their often-misguided coercion into "Star-Performing" leads more to museum curatorial work than that Big Phoenix-Dream-in-the-Sky. And yet we, as teachers, continue to inflict on them the perpetuation of our own taught, in-bred methodology, prolonging the existence of a system almost certain to disappoint and frustrate.

---

* Ibid., CMS: "The New Music Ensemble . . ." (see pg. 37).

Perhaps music educators might come to believe that they could find answers to their problems of relevance by becoming more a part of their artistic society, and by taking an active interest in the contemporary products of the art they serve. The history of Western music has always been typed with this sort of obligation.

The real study of a music student is often abrogated in the pursuit of aping either a professor's words or fingerings, foreseeing a teacher's expectations, or imitating past practices. The technical ability of our performing students is higher than it has ever been in our history; yet I have met so many in my time who, twenty-five years later, were *still* doing the same "exercises," offering work almost precisely the same as they did upon college graduation. During that quarter-century, if we had done our jobs well, those students ought to have had the ability to do transcendental work! Their teaching expertise improved, they became much more facile in their methods of "imitating." In short, they made fewer mistakes now on their path to becoming "master" music teachers; but they knew very little of the real joy and meaning of creation and, in the end, became simply clever jugglers of the stuff of art.

The true study for a music student is more a development of that sensitive side of one's nature, a flowering of the appreciative imagination with which he was so fully endowed when he was a child. Unfortunately, in almost all cases, the contact with the grown-ups shames the song out of him before he has even passed into the real world.

Proposals

I notice that I have spent many minutes with you this morning in what may seem all nay-saying. I told you this was a difficult job for a composer. It is simply that I care so deeply about music education, yet seem to only prove Jacques Barzun's opinion that such discussions are nothing but "one long harangue on everybody's part." I have already indicated possible solutions to some of the problematic issues I have raised; I would now like to most meekly proffer further suggestions for eight of the topics discussed, hopefully to abet the rebirth, from the ashes, of a new Phoenix.

1. *The Government.* Anticipating the "Nation at Risk" reforms, our primary task will undoubtedly be old news to all of you: to keep the arts from being lumped in with "Training for Adulthood" and other general-track courses, to insist that the arts not be dealt savage wounds along with the smorgasbord of electives, that "cafeteria-style curriculum," in the committee's words, that has subverted the traditional academic criteria. People will take us as seriously as we take ourselves.

2. *Art Life at High Tech High.* Our commitment and dedication to counteract what many feel is a disastrous reign of science over our world will only succeed if we incorporate—*mix* the species again—if we fuse the new technology onto our own domain, use it, not oppose it. To contest it is futile; high technology is an edifice built here to stay.

3. *Evolving our own Mythological Beast.* To turn on again the turned-off

students, various mentor programs are now being attempted. Both career guidance and professional role models—those who are *excited* about what they are doing—are the greatest functions of the "outside-world" adults. Educators may itch more at the prospects (the "Contemporary Music Project" program was only scratching the surface) but the linking up of the teacher and the artist, the explainer with the doer, is a mythological beast of a grandly benign design. Both parts must sublimate past differences in a desire to promote the artistic well-being of our youth.

My part of the animal (I don't recall if I'm the head or that other part "behind") has taught me that such a beast cannot be born without an open arm at the school end. I do believe that cooperative artists are eager to share knowledge and, with the teacher's guidance, the students have a rare opportunity. The benefits are not solely artistic, for we can prepare them for living as well as a vocation itself.

4. "*Wobble-Room.*" The enhancement of our future professional cultural life is in direct proportion to the sense of genuine *wonder* and play that we can instill into both secondary school and college students. We need to help pull art back into everyday life. In high schools, we can do more than play recordings and point out an "A-B-A." In colleges, the education of the non-music major could be regarded as a top priority. By using all categories of musics and eliminating the whirlwind "tour-guide" music appreciation mannerisms, the myth that all great music was composed at some high pulpit by white, European males from 1700–1900 only can be dispelled. Furthermore, this now-ingrained glory for the creative imagination may even allow such students, upon becoming grown-ups, to tolerate a fresh new work on a symphony program or opera stage.

In addition, we need to create extra space for, and gather wisdom to stop the current misdirection of, students who now are almost exclusively devoted to the indulgences of their own artistic sensibilities. This is especially problematic with respect to commercial music and jazz programs. We must allow the youngsters to see clearly what the total art world has to offer them and what they must contribute themselves in order for it to serve their own children's needs. The great jazz saxophonist Sonny Rollins remarked that "music is something *beyond* what any human can really own"; to allow playtime for the experience and the depth of Mr. Rollins's sentiment is our mandatory task.

5. *The Media.* I do believe that a collective, solid front of concerned educators could do much to influence this Aural-Armageddon. A unified battle could be waged, without undue conflict, to express our artistic anxieties.

a) Regarding *record stores*, we could attempt to persuade owners that it might possibly be beneficial to: 1) play a short, "classical" piece within their constant commercial juggernaut and 2) exhibit to better effect, even feature, the small independent labels that principally offer the new musics. (I mean, someone might even *buy* it if one could only see or find it!)

b) Regarding *newspapers*, we certainly ought to be able to encourage an expansion of coverage for the arts at least to a level of one-half the space now occupied by high school sports box-score reportage. To date, in my own home town, the activities of world-class, professional musicians often fare much poorer than the high school javelin-thrower; and the former is usually relegated to name-dropping-gossipy columns to boot. A recent issue of *USA Today*, "The Nation's Newspaper," had eighteen pages of sports, with only *six* devoted to "Life": movies, books, music, dancing, art, theater, Hollywood, modeling, elementary psychology, television, and other entertainment. One of those six was a full-page ad for IBM! We can help them do better.

c) Regarding *radio*, would it not be worthwhile to attempt to: 1) strongly encourage business community support for a local classical station, 2) impress upon local non-commercial outlets the need for more new music, more American music, perhaps more live presentations, instead of the Mahler symphonies all of the time, and 3) constantly wage war on behalf of National Public Radio, which is now, as you know, in serious financial trouble?

d) Regarding *television*, the classical music pot is on very low simmer, of course, compared to non-commercial radio's medium-boil. We need to: 1) stress the high priority of the TV medium and encourage musicians to enter the field of television production itself (the musicians need the work); 2) get stations to realize that just panning the orchestra or showing the flute soloist will not attract new viewers. The expertise exemplified by, for example, the Alka-Seltzer or Lite Beer commercials provides a superb yardstick for measuring the meager imagination that now exists on the typical arts-performance show; 3) bring our communal strong-arm to bear on our own institutions to produce and offer the expertise to create videocassette programs, both for instructional use, and also those that would entice the marketing moguls of the educational television stations; 4) redouble our efforts, especially with the appearance of the recent arts channels, to simply render our musicians much more articulate, both generally and about their immediate concerns for their art, in order to preclude a parade of dull master classes and the obtuse ". . . and then I wrote . . ." interviews. A recent showing of a TV meeting with the English sculptor Henry Moore made me realize all over again how absolutely delinquent most musicians are in this respect. Lastly, 5) communicate our most ideal artistic views of *What Ought To Be* to a political hierarchy that allows commercial television to be a two-billion-dollar industry while the non-commercial outlets get by on less than five percent of that.

These few examples of "species-mixing" with media personnel are only cursory. It is not at all a part of my expertise nor, for that matter, my generation's—but I do know that our new Phoenix will die stillborn if we simply continue our present inertia-laden ways. The media is with us to stay—with a vengeance—but educators in classical music circles by and large have not even begun to exploit that industry's unique and powerful potential contributions to our own special industry.

6. *Nurturing an Audience.* Our past and present course of action has predominantly honed in on the "talented" secondary school student. We can

learn to greatly expand our clientele, to remove the caste distinction between student and the citizens of a community. Few have spoken more eloquently about the necessity to provide cultural opportunities for the expanding leisure time of all citizens, young and old, than Charles Leonhard. "Music educators appeared to have retired within the walls of their schools," he says, "pursued their specializations, . . . communicated with their peers rather than the public, and left post-school music on its own."

We are placing self-imposed limits onto people—our prospective auditors —who, when they mature to possess the power to truly aid the planning and organization of professional ensembles, to effectively influence the media with respect to "serious" art—in short, to cause the cultural climate of a specific populace to bloom—these people, it seems, care very little. In effect, we have deserted them when we most needed their help. Community outreach programs, informal pre- and post-concert discussions, municipal performing organizations, "meet the composer" talks, mixing the species of campus and community, taking our own enthusiasm out to attract adult students, are all avenues that we must assiduously tread. The beaming countenance of a sixty-year-old amateur clarinetist following town band jobs in shopping malls, plus his re-introduction to other aspects of local cultural life, is not soon to be forgotten. I know.

7. *Classroom Habits*. The MENC is a powerful lobbying body. It could demand from teacher-training institutions an honest inculcation for their students in the aesthetic imagination of the artists of our own time; i.e., provide for a real study of contemporary art, its failings, successes, and intent. It is downright fatuous of us to expect from students any sympathy for our classical art in the days ahead, when their teachers have not been trained to effectively respond to the philosophic and artistic minds that created it.

Experiments in role-playing, even with very young people, can work well. For example, set up a typical "Arts Council" session: Professor Highsmarts, a TV producer, a Mrs. Very Wealthee, Lawyer Do-Good, a high school choral director, and a local electrician review all the sample arts proposals. They do so in light of attitudes fostered by their varying exposure to music courses. The *mixing of species* allows for a mutual understanding of each other's viewpoint.

Innovative classroom participation in the published "natural sound" compositions is not wasted time, assuming intelligent direction by a teacher who is learned and unafraid. New music doesn't bite! (One of the better works I know is R. M. Schafer's study: passing one sheet of paper around the room. The result? You *listen*!) Better yet, the kids can write their own. Why does it still seem so heretical—usually greeted by the instructor with incredible apprehension—to think that people of all ages can create music the way they now: a) write essays or short stories, b) paint/assemble collage prints or c) sculpt weird mythological beasties of their own? We need to instill creative concepts, not only the *re-creative skills*.

This latter policy can be greatly abetted, both in house and extramurally, by further species-mixing. Team-teaching, or at least sporadic exchanging of the art, drama, music, and literature expertise available, is much discussed but rarely implemented. Also, the teacher's requisite to re-establish cordial relations with those who produce artworks, not only those who write or talk about the products, will not necessarily evolve a hybrid, one-winged Phoenix that is incapable of flight.

Finally, under our classroom considerations, a corollary to our mediations on the general audience, the specialism emphasis. We can back off from developing electives for only those students who already have strong musical backgrounds; we can cease favoring the talented at the expense of the general school population. When funds dwindle and programs are cut (you are all too familiar with that) there is a strong danger that music instruction will lose its fat girth and serve only a segment of the students. For schools will lop off music appreciation before the band or orchestra; they'll delete general music before obliterating the choral program and then we will have an educational home built on sand. Alas, we will have to mix species again: i.e., couple the performance training with the development of an audience to sustain it in the future.

8. *Advocating the New Music.* I said earlier that the composer was not blameless for some of the gap existing between himself and his listeners. The anticipated single-pot, that synthesis of contemporary music into "the new style," so long espoused by many, has evolved instead into a salad bowl that appears permanent. Many composers, breaking away from the postwar hold of the forties and fifties, are now producing personal, direct, heartfelt, yet diverse statements defying classification. They are supplanting analysis of progress-in-art with simply the experience of the music itself. A good sign, it seems, for it bodes well for us as educators too.

The art-atrophy, the museum seen by leading musicians like Bernstein and Foss, the massive neglect of excellent twentieth-century music in both school and professional concert programs must be censured—and strongly so—by our collective sense of mission. And we can do so without pointing the finger. We can make a different attitude prevail, or at least make those others responsible for the prevailing mood think thrice.

Outside of academia, professional performing artists and planners are not fulfilling their obligation to the grand art they purport to serve if they are not energetically dedicated to the worthwhile music of our century. I suggest that a collaborative assault by educators on the leading performing artists of our time, and their managers, would not be met with careless or unreasoning objections.

Within the schools, encouragement for music competitions, commissions, workshops, prizes, the sponsoring of new music events aimed at all our people, irrespective of age or interest, would at least enhance the present abysmal quality of much educational music and also help allow today's weirdo-lunatic composer to be perceived as a caring, communicative human.

One cannot mechanize a "now" creative art. One cannot institutionalize our time's imaginative dreams without their wearing out, running down like Hans Christian Andersen's mechanical nightingale. For the real nightingale, like our new Phoenix, will return. We can help the latter's rebirth from its ashes. It will make the difference.

Coda

Heywood Broun said that "no body politic is healthy until it begins to itch." The present condition of American musical education in relation to the artistic temperament it serves need not always be what it is today. There is nothing inviolate about the status quo. Music education can be altered as little or as much as we choose. Its continued scratching, good health could be guaranteed by enhancing the aesthetic and intellectual well-being of its constituents and easily destroyed by just continuing to feed upper classes with more instrumentalists and singers; wiped out by adding its share to fostering public schools which grow contented neighbors and worthy civilians rather than developing one's innate brilliance and nurturing principles for the study of the art of mankind. We must tend to our students' dreams and fancies, their imaginative-receptive powers, in order to prevent the art we so cherish from dying away. For, after its death—following the Phoenix ashes—remember these words of Carl Sandburg from "Remembrance Rock":

> The shroud has no pockets.
> The dead hold in their clenched hands
> only that which they have given away.

It is a premise with me—one I have consistently believed in and have tried to act upon all my life—that we cannot deny our country's youth the kind of musical, aesthetic, and artistic education they ought to get. They deserve it. We, you and I, owe it to them. I don't care how we do it, but we have to do it and do it right.

The few proposals hinted at herein are only ideas, not plans. Not unlike the species-mixing of the mythical beasts, we need to amalgamate the caring artist with the knowledgeable educator and administrator to evolve such ideas into a plan: a plan blending our beliefs together, mirroring our honesty—in sum, becoming us. *We* are the plan. It is idealistic, of course, but we were born that way. Man was foreordained to act thus, to confirm by our acts the value of our goals and persist in so affirming—i.e., to make an ideal. An open dialogue and literature, the thrashing-through, with friendly savagery, of the aesthetic and pragmatic dilemmas that exist between student, citizen, teacher, and artist will reincarnate our Phoenix. From the ashes it will rise, a novel creature growing into the fantastic new Phoenix and flying for the next triumphant years.

Contemporary biology has taught us that it is the way of the world for living things to join up, establish linkages, live inside one another, return to earlier arrangements, get along, whenever possible.

Any animal, dear colleagues—whether insect, fish, fowl, or man—brought into contact with another, however foreign, will fuse with it, given the opportunity and the right conditions. It will become, for a time anyway, a single cell, ready to dance . . . ready to multiply. It is a Phoenix. It is an omen of good fortune. It is a wish for our future world, yours and mine.

Summary of Group Discussions

The reactions of discussion group members to Sydney Hodkinson's speech were diverse and often quite lively. Hodkinson's address not only illuminated his perceptions of the state of contemporary music in education and society, but also raised a number of additional issues of fundamental importance to music educators. These issues included questions of performance, teaching, understanding, and priorities which speak to the very heart of what music education is (or perhaps should be) about.

The overemphasis on "common practice period" materials in the musical training of treachers was identified. Contemporary music was said to often be treated as distinct from the music of other eras. This distinction may be justified since contemporary music is "what's happening now," but it does not justify ignoring it; in doing so, a major aspect of contemporary culture is also ignored. Several participants suggested the need for greater exposure of prospective teachers to contemporary music and current compositional techniques. This increased exposure might manifest itself in more diversified theory courses, performances, listening, and compositional experiences. All seemed to agree that teacher training in this area is at best inadequate and that the route to a greater appreciation of contemporary music is paved with musical understanding and experience.

The need for increased communication and contact between educators, composers, and publishers was a common thread in many of the discussions. These three groups tend to blame each other for both the lack of suitable contemporary literature and the overabundance of published works of questionable quality.

The practical considerations and limitations of teachers in the field were also discussed. Many teachers, working under pressures of public performances and contests, feel they have little or no available time to devote to the teaching of contemporary music. This concern generated further discussion focusing on the identification of priorities for music teaching and learning. Some participants felt that performance is overemphasized and is thus detrimental to the teaching of a wide range of musical knowledge and skills. An opposing opinion was that performance is among the best methods for presenting musical concepts to students. The comprehensive musicianship approach, utilizing aspects of both views, was suggested by one group member as a solution to this problem.

Further disagreement arose concerning the presentation and use of contemporary music in elementary and secondary schools. Some felt that it might be important to expose students to contemporary music but questioned the use of such music for performance due to a lack of understanding on the part of audiences. This also raised the related issue of the music teacher's responsibility to his or her students or to an audience. The use of program notes with clear explanations was recommended as a solution to this problem, one which haunts the professional as well as academic music worlds.

Several group members disagreed with Hodkinson's comment that re-creative behavior is not imaginative. These participants felt that this type of behavior, when manifested through performance, allows imaginative and creative musical interpretations.

The issues raised in Hodkinson's address were both controversial and compelling. Conference participants expressed admiration for his views and many seemed genuinely moved by his passionate speech. A major point of agreement was the expression of an urgent need for tearing down artificial barriers which restrict free communication of ideas and opinions among composers, performers, educators, and audiences.

Music: Basic Education

WILLARD L. BOYD

Our future depends upon our creativity and our time. As our physical resources become less plentiful, we must rely more heavily on human resources —our creative selves.

During the 1980s, creativity must be fostered. The arts and humanities must be stressed as well as the sciences. Arms do not guarantee international security. Longer life and cleaner air do not assure happiness. Ideas and ideals, understanding and sensitivity give meaning to life. Because there are limits to material growth, we must concentrate on other means of development and fulfillment.

We must use the time of our lives creatively. The next decade is expected to be a period of career difficulties for many. There is fear of an over-educated, under-employed population. If we are to flourish, we must multiply our personal interests. We must restructure our lives to encompass the satisfaction of volunteerism and leisure as well as paid work. If this is so, we will come to value the whole of our lives. If a nation is willing to look at the whole of its potential, it can view the future with confidence.

Americans esteem education as the most effective means of human development. Education is perennially and naively viewed as the panacea for all national ills; we can solve any American problem if we include it in the curriculum. Competition for educational time is fierce and only the most pressing national priorities can be addressed. Currently, commission after commission is urging greater educational attention to science and mathematics in order to maintain American leadership.

The arts in education have not been a national priority for the melting pot Americans. Ironically, the arts have always been prominent in the lives of Native Americans and also in the lives of ethnic people who followed our first European settlers. Song, dance, and cultural crafts were common to those inhabiting the North American continent in the sixteenth and seventeenth centuries and they have been vital in the lives of Hispanics, blacks, and other groups who settled in America in subsequent centuries.

While on one hand, John Adams, in his time, placed the arts last in his nation-building priorities; on the other hand, W. E. B. DuBois, in his time, ranked black song and story a more significant contribution to the nation than black toil.

At long last, the arts are flourishing in the United States, and they are flourishing everywhere in the United States. Since 1965, the number of professional arts associations has grown by almost 700 percent. The number of professional orchestras has increased from 58 to 145; professional opera companies from 30 to 109; professional dance companies from 35 to 250; and professional theater companies from 40 to 500. As the number of artistic groups grew, so did audiences. In 1965, for example, about one million tickets were sold for dance performances, chiefly in New York City. Today, there are about sixteen million ticket buyers for dance performances, and 90 percent of them live outside New

York. Similarly, the audience for orchestras has risen from 10 million to 23 million. Average annual attendance at museums of art has gone from 22 million to more than 43 million.

Americans are coming to value the arts as they do education. We must forge a connection between the arts and education.

Since human creativity constitutes a nation's greatest wealth, education must always address the needs of the gifted and the talented. That national wealth must be shared with all citizens through general education. The arts and education are an essential ingredient of our future creativity and fulfillment. Universal education must include the arts in order to nurture talent and to extend artistic appreciation to the general citizenry. This is not an easy task to accomplish.

The role of arts education in the United States is now embroiled in the argument about "basic skills" as well as fiscal priorities. The popular cry is for a "return to basics" in education. Our school curriculum, it is said, contains too many frills, too many luxuries of excessive cost and dubious educational value. Many think the argument is about what subjects should be taught—a good deal of the argument is really about how well we are teaching the subjects now in the curricula. Frequently, however, those who wield the budgetary or scholastic knife make their first cut in the arts.

The National Commission on Excellence in Education recommends ". . . that state and local high school graduation requirements be strengthened and that, at a minimum, all students seeking a diploma be required to lay the foundations in the 'Five New Basics' by taking the following curriculum during their four years of high school: a) four years of English; b) three years of mathematics; c) three years of science; d) three years of social studies; and e) one-half year of computer science.

"For the college-bound, two years of foreign language in high school are strongly recommended in addition to those taken earlier."

"Whatever the student's educational or work objectives, knowledge of the New Basics is the foundation of success for the after-school years, and, therefore, forms the core of the modern curriculum. A high level of shared education in these basics, together with work in the fine and performing arts and foreign languages, constitutes the mind and spirit of our culture . . ."

The Commission goes on to state:

> The high school curriculum should also provide students with programs requiring rigorous effort in subjects that advance students' personal, educational, and occupational goals, such as the fine and performing arts and vocational education. These areas complement the New Basics and they should demand the same level of performance as the basics.

> The curriculum in the crucial eight grades leading to the high school years should be specifically designed to provide a sound base for study in those and later years in such areas as English language development and writing, computational and problem-solving skills, science, social studies, foreign language, and the arts. These years should foster an enthusiasm for learning and the development of the individual's gifts and talents.

The College Board has prescribed six basic academic subjects for high school students who intend to go to college. The subjects are English, mathematics, science, social studies, foreign language, and the arts.

According to the College Board,

> Students going to college will profit from the following preparation in the arts:
> • The ability to understand and appreciate the unique qualities of each of the arts.
> • The ability to appreciate how people of various cultures have used the arts to express themselves.
> • The ability to understand and appreciate different artistic styles and works from representative historical periods and cultures.
> • Some knowledge of the social and intellectual influences affecting artistic form.
> • The ability to use the skills, media, tools, and processes required to express themselves in one or more of the arts.
>
> College entrants also will profit from more intensive preparation in at least one of the four areas of the arts: visual arts, theater, music, and dance.

*   *   *

> If the preparation of college entrants is in music, they will need the following knowledge and skills.
> • The ability to identify and describe—using the appropriate vocabulary—various musical forms from different historical periods.
> • The ability to listen perceptively to music, distinguishing such elements as pitch, rhythm, timbre, and dynamics.
> • The ability to read music.
> • The ability to evaluate a musical work or performance.
> • To know how to express themselves by playing an instrument, singing in a group or individually, or composing music.

It is encouraging that the arts are included in the current curricular debates. To make them central to curriculum will require our strenuous advocacy.

Like most basic skills and fundamental education, very little is known about the arts. I view the arts as a basic form of communication comparable to, but different from, the words of language and the symbols of mathematics.

The arts meet a basic human need: creative personal expression. In addition to their intrinsic value, the arts give insights into other aspects of life, helping people understand themselves and the world in which they live. It is recognized that quality education should include the development of skills, knowledge, concepts, values, and sensitivities with which to understand and engage the culture of a nation. The arts offer significant opportunities for this development. Learning must incorporate the arts as a central, significant, and integral component. Artistic and educational institutions must recognize and support this concept. The arts can greatly enrich our lives and in so doing have basic value.

The question becomes, then, how best to emphasize the mutual benefits of the arts and education. There are many answers to this question, many valid responses, but each echoes a single conclusion: The artistic and educational communities must join together to foster artistic excellence in performance and appreciation.

The quality of the arts in education depends ultimately upon the talented teacher working with the creative student. Students are inspired by individual teachers rather than administrative systems. Exceptional teachers, like exceptional artistry, requires great talent. Therefore, colleges and universities must be concerned with the preparation of outstanding arts educators at all levels of instruction. Quite simply, excellent teachers are indispensable to the training of artists and to the advancement of arts among the citizenry.

Such teaching talent must be cultivated through preparation and continuous development. This involves pre-service and in-service training and development for four general kinds of arts educators: 1) arts specialists, 2) artists, 3) general classroom teachers, and 4) non-traditional teachers and aides.

1. *Arts Specialists in Elementary-Secondary Schools.* Artistic creativity is the moving force in arts education. Pre-service training for arts specialists for the schools should focus on artistic as well as teaching creativity. Much is required of the arts specialist. He or she must first be an exceptional teacher, excelling in at least one art form. Like the science teacher, the arts specialist must understand the interrelationship among the arts and between the arts and other subjects. The arts specialist must serve both the vocational and avocational needs of a variety of students, from the casually interested to the prospective professional. She or he must often serve as a rallying point, incorporating artists and artistic organizations into teaching programs, and enlisting the commitment of classroom teachers, school administrators, parents, and the public to the importance of the arts in education.

The preparation of this virtuoso requires a catholic yet demanding tertiary educational and training program. Such a program should emphasize artistic creativity. This focus must be accompanied by an understanding of the learning process, student motivation, teaching techniques, curriculum construction, community resources, and the relative merits of disciplinary and interdisciplinary approaches. All of this requires imaginative as well as rigorous teacher preparation which emphasizes the inseparability of fine arts and teacher training curricula.

Like teachers of science and mathematics, arts teachers must continue to develop. Schools, colleges, and universities must provide opportunities for arts specialists to pursue the study and practice of their artistic disciplines. Residencies, fellowships, teacher exchanges, and leaves of absence are the means needed to assure that specialists can return to study and creative activity. Such study should broaden and deepen arts and teaching skills and encourage utilization of arts resources, team teaching, interdisciplinary studies, and teaching special constituencies. Teaching artists should be given released time to execute commissioned works, to serve as artists-in-schools, and to pursue independent study and work. School systems should experiment with special leaves for gifted specialists, and training institutions should have some residency and fellowship money designated for such specialists.

2. *Artists.* To some extent, and if only by the example their work represents, all artists teach. Throughout their schooling and training, artists should be

made aware of the variety of teaching opportunites open to them. They should be given a sense of the special creative demands and rewards of teaching. Artists in training might learn something of this by interning as aides to arts specialists.

Professional artists who are involved for a limited period of teaching can greatly enrich the arts education program of a school or arts institution. They can aid in the identification of talented students and stimulate the interest of general students. Their thoughtful incorporation into the arts program can make clear to students the unity of purpose between teachers and artists. Mutual respect and trust among the regular arts faculty, the artists in residence, and the school administration are important requirements in such cooperative ventures. Workshops and seminars are an invaluable preparation for the artist who will assume this instructional role, either during the training years or subsequently as a part of the career development. Conversely, such workshops can be stimulating to the arts specialist who works with the teaching artist.

3. *Elementary School Teachers.* Enormous demands are placed on elementary classroom teachers. As generalists, they are expected to teach all the basic skills for life and learning. To teach content, they must know something about each subject area.

The arts must be a vital part of the elementary school curriculum. Teaching in elementary schools is done best by those who can take a personal interest in the young child. This requires the involvement of the general classroom teacher as well as the arts specialist. In their preparation, all elementary teachers should become comfortable in their understanding, appreciation, and use of the arts, so that they can bring aesthetic awareness to the general class and help identify talented young people. To the extent possible, their preparation as teachers should include exposure to at least one art form, to artists, and to arts curricula. In-service training can enhance the arts in the elementary curriculum and assist teachers throughout their teaching career.

4. *Teachers and Volunteers in Cultural Institutions.* At long last we are becoming aware of the inseparability of cultural and educational institutions. We are recognizing that educational institutions are cultural and that cultural institutions are educational. Both institutions are vitally concerned with the arts.

Cultural institutions do more than enrich; they strengthen basic skills, basic knowledge, basic comprehension, and basic understanding. Cultural institutions educate, and each year are educating more and more people. Their audiences, their students, are of all ages and all backgrounds. They reach students in a variety of circumstances and a variety of times. Cultural institutions along with educational institutions develop people.

In cultural institutions, learning occurs by calculation as well as serendipity. More and more cultural institutions are engaged in conscious teaching of even the occasional visitor or member of the audience.

We must be concerned with the preparation and development of the increasing number of teachers in cultural institutions. A variety of talented and dedicated individuals serve the educational mission of cultural institutions and groups either as paid or volunteer teachers or aides. A new type of career is emerging which requires both pre- and in-service training. These non-school educators may be prepared as traditional teachers or they may require a different preparation.

Regardless of forum or format, excellence in arts education depends upon the identification, preparation, and development of talented teachers. As teachers they must be concerned with both gifted students and the general student. This concern must follow the student beyond elementary and secondary education. Arts education must also be a vital part of tertiary and continuing education.

In the United States, there is an increasing involvement of colleges and universities in arts education. Admission policies are being modified to recognize artistic talent as a significant variable in college entrance requirements. These admission criteria determine course offerings in secondary schools, and should include the arts in prerequisites, grade point averages, aptitude tests, and other relevant considerations.

American colleges and universities are offering instructional programs to prepare professional artists, arts educators, and general arts majors or minors who, like students in physics, political science, zoology, or history, wish to combine the arts with other studies to prepare for broad employment opportunities in the private or public sector. In the face of increasing career uncertainties, we should not consider a major in the arts any less valuable preparation for graduate work or entry into employment than majors offered in the humanities and sciences.

Most American colleges and universities are currently reviewing their general education requirements. We can take satisfaction that a major outcome of these reviews is to include the arts as a distribution requirement.

Moreover, as education is increasingly recognized as a continuing process not limited to people between eighteen and twenty-one years old, educational and artistic institutions must be concerned with these continuing needs. Formal and informal programs for citizens of all ages can extend the arts into the lives of many who are not now either artist or audience. Local institutions can respond to the artistic needs of their communities, while art centers and universities can serve larger geographical areas. This is done in a variety of ways: through art appreciation courses; through stages, museums, and concert halls. As an assembly of talented students and faculty, American universities and colleges are among the nation's foremost patrons of artistic creativity. In addition, many of our universities serve as impresario and sponsor artistic programs drawing talent from throughout the nation.

Through education at all levels, and in a variety of places, we must develop discerning audiences. Greater public appreciation and access to the arts will enhance both citizen and artist. Education in arts is the best way to ensure the building of appreciative audiences; mere exposure to the arts does not create more discerning audiences. Three recent American studies in the development of arts audiences indicate that general education alone is a vital factor.

Now is the time for us to be effective advocates for the arts in our education.

Both the arts and education are principally matters of local policy and finance. Nevertheless, there must be national concern for creativity and education. That national concern must be addressed by the artistic as well as the educational community. The National Endowment for the Arts must be actively involved. The mission of the National Endowment for the Arts in education is one of advocacy and assessment. The NEA can play an important role in encouraging state and local arts agencies to work with state and local school boards in advancing the arts in education. The NEA has an obligation to be an active catalyst in this process. The National Science Foundation speaks to the importance of science and mathematics in curriculum. The National Endowment for the Humanities speaks to the importance of the humanities in the curriculum. The National Endowment for the Arts must speak to the importance of arts in education.

The basic advocacy of arts education will always be local. It will require the commitment of artists and the commitment of citizens. Most of all it will require the commitment of arts teachers. They must be involved at all levels of strategy and advocacy. Their professional organizations must be aggressive in competing for curricular priority in a time of educational retrenchment and reallocation. Arts teachers must be assertive in studying the agenda for in-service teacher training whenever it takes place. If the school district is unionized, arts educators must be sure that the bargaining representatives understand the importance of the arts in education.

Arts educators must be venturesome. They must not be defensive. They must cooperate enthusiastically with artists and cultural institutions. They must be imaginative in relating to and developing new audiences and constituencies. Most of all arts educators must be open-minded and open to all.

As educators, artists, and public we must open our lives to the arts so that our lives can be opened by the arts. For as two friends of mine once said, in a joint statement upon receiving a citation at the Iowa State Fair:

> Pictures—many of them—have shed their frames.
>
> This goes for all the arts. Theater is out of its proscenium frame and into the street. Sculpture is off the pedestal and into the landscape—in fact, it has become landscape. "Everything we do is music," says John Cage. "Everywhere is the best seat."
>
> Likewise, our community is no longer framed by the city limits or national borders. It is our environment and our earth. It is never-ending— and you can't frame that.
>
> For some of us this is release—exhilarating! For some it is a threat. Maybe, at times, each of us misses the comfort of familiar home territory within our accustomed frame.
>
> You remember, perhaps, a film of three African lions being given their freedom. The crates in which they traveled were opened. Their liberators waited for the exultant moment. The kings of the jungle wouldn't budge. Like many humans they preferred the safety of their frames. They were threatened by new freedom.
>
> Too many humans are wasting themselves and others because we cling to the old frames. Too many in their fear of changed horizons throw up new bound-

aries, new frames—those of the ghetto, the suburb, overkill, nuclear paranoia.

Like artists of the past, ours are giving us the symbols with which to cope in this twentieth-century landscape. If we can envision successful living on this endangered planet, we can achieve it:

Our arts and our living are one and the same. We too must feel a part of our environment, sense the flow between ourselves and the landscape, live in the street rather than behind locked doors, realize that everything we do is music. We must shed our frames.

If we shed our frames, the arts can help us meet our uncertain future with confidence.

Summary of Group Discussions

There was a general feeling in the discussion groups that the tone of Boyd's speech had been refreshingly positive and optimistic. There are many fine teachers in music education, but it always seems easier to spotlight the negative. One discussion leader suggested that music educators always "pick their scabs" regarding the state of the profession. We too often forget that America trains many of the world's top musicians, and the success of our public music education programs is the envy of the rest of the world.

General concern was expressed regarding the preparation of both music specialists and elementary classroom teachers for teaching music. As most artists end up being educators in some form, we must foster an interest among them in learning how to teach. Although many are willing to go into the public schools, lack of financial reward is a stumbling block. Federal and trust funds, although increasingly scarce, are available to encourage such work. One panelist had sent letters to members of his community in order to commission a work for his school ensemble. Another pointed out that museum staff members are often able and willing to aid in fund raising for the purpose of placing artists in the schools.

Low pay and negative peer pressure from fellow artists who portray teaching as a less important use of talent than "performing" tend to discourage artists from entering teaching as a full-time profession. We must find ways to encourage qualified people to enter the education field. Those who are already in the field must take responsibility for improving themselves through personal reading and research, and not wait for a course or conference in order to move forward.

More than one participant questioned the effectiveness of our current public school music teachers. One of our primary tasks is to produce educated consumers of music, but research has shown little correlation between public school music training and concert attendance. Another pointed out that early motivational influences are too varied to adequately measure, but churches are too often overlooked. Private teachers are also very important, perhaps more so than public school teachers. At least, this is the impression that successful performers often give. Actually, the public school teacher often encourages the student to begin private study. Perhaps there should be a coalition between public and private teachers, as many studio teachers have no contact with educational institutions.

Are teachers less effective now than in the past? Many politicians and media people say yes, perhaps realizing that this makes a great issue. Actually, it is impossible to compare the present with the past. The social problems have changed as the intellectual demands of the world have increased, and children are different as well. Furthermore, we still do not know what qualities an effective teacher needs.

Fewer of today's music students, it was suggested, are taking private lessons, and students do not show up as consistently for extra rehearsals. It is often the case that music directors are at least partly at fault for the latter problem, making unreasonable time demands of their students. It is questionable whether a large amount of school time should be taken for cultural field trips, music assemblies, and private lessons.

There are important ways in which programs have fallen short of their potential. Teachers of ensembles, which constitute the majority of secondary music classes, devote too large a percentage of their time to the preparation of performances. Music involves thought as well as skill, and one of our primary tasks is to teach students how to think. For what we are actually accomplishing, secondary music may, in fact, be getting too great an amount of schedule time. On the other hand, music classes are often too large for adequate coverage of their subject matter, and overfill their physical facilities. From situations such as these future music majors graduate with deficiencies in non-performance skills such as music history and theory. Directors could in part alleviate these problems by taking a comprehensive approach in high school ensemble rehearsals, although community and administrative pressures for such activities as marching band often dictate the use of rehearsal time.

Creativity is not a goal limited to teachers. The important creative side of music-making must be shared with students. Experiences in composition and improvisation should be a part of every student's background. The question was raised as to whether these tasks are facets of the same skill. There seem to be too few spontaneous music-makers in the typical classroom.

The issue of testing in music commanded a large amount of discussion time. The purposes of testing are to evaluate instruction, to aid students in self-evaluation, and to provide the public with the data it demands. Music educators avoid testing, however, because music—and skills in general—are hard to measure. Testing implies the existence of hard and fast "rules," but such rules may not be in the nature of the "open" subject of music. Testing also creates pressure on students.

A participant observed that the aesthetic experience, while not unique to the arts, is one of the arts' most important contributions to education. Contrary to the impression that arts educators may have helped to foster, aesthetic experience is part of everyone's life, and should be part of each person's basic decision-making process. We must draw attention to the whole, rather than to the parts alone.

On the technological side, we must make use of the tools—such as the computer—which science has given us. Scientists often revere and enrich their lives through music, but how many music educators do the same through science?

Among the benefits of the conference which participants pointed out was the exposure it provided to progressive ideas through its "current" and provocative speakers. Practitioners in the field often lack such stimulation. One of the major changes which they felt the symposium would engender was a greater focus on the music student as a whole person, rather than only as a performer. It was felt that the participants in the symposium carried a great deal of responsibility for change by virtue of having been in attendance.

The Future of Musical Education in America: A Pragmatist's View

CHARLES LEONHARD

The level of segmentation in the professions allied with music would indicate that a professional music educator involved with music teacher education should limit his remarks on the future of musical education in America to the public school program and music teacher education. My broad definition of music education as an enterprise encompassing all deliberate efforts to develop musicianship regardless of the level at which they take place, and my conviction that a positive future for the public school music program and the music teacher education program requires an overhaul of the entire enterprise of musical education, preclude such a limitation.

As a music educator who is also a pragmatist, I seek to analyze musical education in America, identify weaknesses in the enterprise and ask the pragmatic question: What difference would a given course of action make in remedying the weaknesses identified? This effort provides the focus of this paper. I shall identify weaknesses, suggest courses of action, and project the results of changes.

The Circularity of Music Programs

Several limiting conditions pertain to the musical establishment in the United States that inevitably affect the future of musical education in America. The first is the circularity of music programs in the public schools on the one hand and in colleges and universities on the other. Collegiate institutions prepare music teachers who go out to prepare music students, through private and school instruction, to become students in collegiate institutions. The musical horizons, skills, and attitudes of music students entering collegiate institutions are shaped by their public school and private teachers at the collegiate level. Any limitations in the preparation of music teachers are inevitably passed on to the students of those teachers. It all boils down to a vicious circle which can only be broken at the collegiate level. Critics of public school music teachers must recognize that most of their deficiencies are directly traceable to the collegiate institution that prepared them.

The Chasm Between Art Music and Popular Music

A second condition is the unfortunate and unjustified chasm that has developed in this country between art music and popular and ethnic musics. The art of music is a gestalt consisting of a variety of styles, all of which have one thing in common: they illuminate our life of feeling and have a profound effect on our human potential.

The American music establishment and the public have, however, apparently failed to recognize and appreciate the unifying factors in musical expression. Art music has become the domain of the privileged and operates as a divisive rather than a unifying force in the society. We have separated art music from life and approach its performance as a cultural ritual rather than as a glorification of life. Concert behavior of both performers and listeners has become overly stylized and ritualistic. Regrettably, a similar ritualistic dogma has even come to pervade concerts by the symphonic band.

The only exceptions arise in programs of the Boston Pops, and at some of the summer festivals where audiences come to celebrate life and to enjoy music representing a variety of styles with a glass of wine in hand and the freedom to respond in ways that suit them and are appropriate to the expressive import of the music. Pearl Bailey and her songs and patter are juxtaposed with the performance of Mozart and Brahms.

The Limited Scope of Student Experiences with Music

A third condition, the limited scope of musical experiences gained by students in schools and colleges reinforces, if it does not create, the dichotomy between traditional art music and contemporary art music and between art music and popular and ethnic musics. In school listening programs at all levels students learn simply to tolerate rather than respond to traditional art music, much of which is over their heads emotionally and intellectually. Any attention the teacher gives to popular music occurs as a sop to what the elite and the pseudo-elite consider the unfortunate taste of the masses.

The musical diet of collegiate music majors is limited to art music of the seventeenth, eighteenth, and nineteenth centuries with only infrequent and often disdainful nods to ethnic and popular music. Even jazz, recognized all over the world as an authentic American art form, has only recently gained a small and often precarious foothold in college music programs.

Examination of college catalogues reveals that most departments and schools of music would more properly be called schools or departments of seventeenth, eighteenth, and nineteenth century music. The great bulk of the program in both performance and theoretical studies has to do with these three centuries in the history of music. Stravinsky is often the latest of the great composers to receive systematic attention.

The last sixty years in the development of music have had dismayingly small impact on the content of college music programs. Contemporary art music is a no man's land for the majority of students at most collegiate institutions. Even such giants as Varèse and Stockhausen, not to mention Cage and other living American composers, are often unknown quantities. Attention to popular and ethnic musics is practically nonexistent except for isolated courses in ethnomusicology.

Needless to say, the programs of established performing groups, both public and collegiate, reflect this limited scope. The failure of public school and college music programs to initiate music students and general students into music other than the standard repertory has resulted in a level of conservatism in the preferences of the broad music audience that is not characteristic of audiences for the other arts. George Balanchine, Martha Graham, and Merce Cunningham have literally transformed the face of dance in this country; no composer since Stravinsky has been able to budge the music establishment from its traditional stance, and his acceptance sprang from France. One wonders what would have happened had he lived his whole life in the United States.

The Homogeneity of College Music Program

A fourth limiting condition is found in the homogeneity of college music programs. Every school and department of music, aided and abetted by the National Association of Schools of Music, has sought to assume the roles of music programs in the conservatory tradition, the liberal arts tradition, and the teachers college tradition regardless of the quality and extent of its resources. Small departments emulate large ones; mediocre departments emulate distinguished ones. As a result, thousands of music students have been graduated with inferior undergraduate and graduate degrees in applied music and composition (the conservatory tradition), in music history and theory (the liberal arts tradition), and in music teacher education (the teachers college tradition). Very few college music administrators and faculties have been sufficiently courageous and realistic to ask such questions as: What programs are consistent with the needs of the existing clientele for music instruction? Do we have the resources required to offer a quality graduate program? And, how many mediocre pianists does the country really need?

The Status of Music Administration

The administration of music programs at both collegiate and public school levels is in need of serious attention. College music administrators often assume responsibility for operations involving hundreds of thousands or millions of dollars without having been initiated into the art and science of administration through academic preparation or apprenticeship. A composer, performer, or musicologist tonight; a music administrator tomorrow morning. The frequent result is a level of ineptness in fiscal, facilities, and personnel management that would not be tolerated for a day in a commercial operation.

In the public schools the passing years have seen the steady erosion in the authority of music administrators. They are now rarely given the title of director, which implies responsibility for the total program and requisite authority to carry out that responsibility; they frequently bear the title of consultant and their positions are often as anomalous as the title. The great school music programs of the past were brought about by the likes of Mabelle Glenn in Kansas City, Russell Morgan in Cleveland, Fowler Smith in Detroit, T. P. Giddings in Minneapolis and Louis Wersen in Philadelphia. They were sure of their power and authority; they had the support of the commercial and cultural establishment; they had access to the seats of power in their city; and they promoted a comprehensive program of music education without fear or favor.

The Lack of Unity

The enterprises of musical education, and the music and arts community generally, are marked by divisiveness and competition when they should be unified and mutually supportive. We have myriad organizations all with benign motives: MENC, NASM, ABDA, CBDNA, ACDA, NAJE, the Orff Association, the Kodály Association, the Alliance for Arts Education, the Arts Alliance, the Art Coalition and Arts Councils, each plowing its own row and never forming a cohesive force for political and social action in support of the arts and arts education.

The Public School Program

Conditions in the public school music program also merit recognition in any consideration of the future of musical education in America. The openness of the public school curriculum over the last fifty years, and the relative prosperity of the country between 1950 and 1975 with a concomitant high level of funding for public schools, provided fertile ground for the development of the public school music program. School administrators were willing to hire and the public willing to support music specialists at every level of the public school music program. It became commonplace for millions of students to participate in performance groups on a daily schedule often with full academic credit.

Twin forces, a depressed economy and the general disillusionment of the public with education as a whole, have generated the old cry of "Back to Basics" and resulted in cutbacks in music programs. The problem is exacerbated by the continuing reduction in the number of school age children and young people.

For music education, as is true for all of education, the fulsomeness of the fifties and sixties has vanished. We, too, along with John Kennedy and Martin Luther King, Jr., had a dream, and were confident of our ability to bring music to every child and produce a musically educated public unique in the history of the world. That dream is far from reality, and music teachers are among the first to go when financial problems strike the schools.

Alarm over falling test scores, portentous pronouncements of such bodies as the President's Commission on Excellence in Education, practices in college admissions, and crises in financing public schools have combined to threaten the place of music in the public school program along with other subjects considered less than solid by traditionalists.

The positions of music specialists in elementary schools are being abolished or threatened in many districts; college-bound high school students are being increasingly counseled out of performance groups into mathematics, science, computer, and language courses; opportunities for students to take elective courses are being reduced; college admissions officers are ever more scornful of credit in music along with credit in art and psychology.

A public school music program characterized by sparsity of music specialists in the elementary schools, limited opportunities for students to develop performance skills in elementary and junior high school, and decreased participation in high school performance groups appears to be imminent.

Implications for Change

Each of the limitations in musical education previously cited provides a basis for deriving implications for change which will make a positive difference in the quality of education in music students receive and, as a consequence, contribute to the health of musical education and the American music establishment:

1. The circularity of collegiate, public school, and private instruction in music must be recognized by all parties concerned and involved with musical education. Professors of music in collegiate institutions need to become acquainted with the problems of public school music educators, work with them to identify deficiencies in the preparation of music teachers, and become involved with the total program of musical education. Only then can appropriate changes in collegiate programs and public school program occur. The logical agents for change in the broad music scene are the collegiate institutions; only they can break the circle to achieve change.

2. Collegiate institutions will put their forces to work to bridge the chasm between art music and popular and ethnic musics. Hiring faculty members whose preparation diverges from the traditional academic preparation and who themselves exemplify the bridging of the gap is essential. Accomplishing this change will require moderating the mania for advanced academic degrees which characterizes all but a few major collegiate institutions. How can one justify the doctor's degree having become almost a union card for membership on a college music faculty? Music administrators have been remiss in not establishing with higher administrators that artistic performance qualifications are as important as, and frequently more important than, academic qualifications. For example, an instrumentalist who combines skill in performing jazz and popular music with skill in performing art music, with his or her credentials established through a combination of professional experience and academic preparation, can contribute greatly to bridging the chasm between art music and popular music, and to helping students develop a broad orientation to the unity of musical expression.

3. Conductors of collegiate performing groups will cease aping the ritualistic approach to performance followed by professional symphony conductors. They will program concerts with a wide variety of musical styles including traditional art music, contemporary music including experimental efforts, and popular music. Broader programming along with a greater degree of informality in dress and presentation and "color commentary," by the conductor or another knowledgeable person, will be helpful in educating the public and performers. All conductors should take note of the educative role of commentators in televised sports events. As a result of those commentators, millions of Americans have developed an impressive level of discrimination concerning the quality of play and coaching strategy. Would that we develop in the common man a comparable level of discrimination with regard to differences in musical styles and quality of performance.

4. Collegiate institutions will make instruction in, and performance of, popular music, folk music, ethnic music, and jazz an integral part of the music program. Able performers of those styles of music will become members of musical faculties as jazz musicians have done in some institutions.

5. Contemporary American composers will be brought into the main-

stream of the musical and academic life of public schools and colleges. Their compositions will be performed by all types of school and college groups and heard by the general public, not just by other composers and a small coterie of devotees to contemporary idioms.

Graduates of such a broadened program will pass their enhanced perspective of music on to their students who will later come to the collegiate institutions with anticipation of, and preparation for, an education in the broad spectrum of music as it exists in the real world. The face of musical education and the character of the broad music establishment could be changed in one generation.

6. Collegiate institutions will take steps to moderate the stultifying homogeneity that characterizes music programs throughout the country. Institutions emphasizing the conservatory tradition to prepare professional performers will be limited to schools with musical resources comparable to those found at Eastman, Juilliard, and a few megauniversities. A few such programs of high quality can prepare a sufficient number of concert artists, symphony players, opera singers, composers, and conductors to fulfill the needs of the country. A well-organized national program designed to identify young musicians with outstanding talent, and to funnel them *with financial assistance* to appropriate institutions, represents an essential corollary. (A job for the National Endowment for the Arts?)

Similarly, programs designed to offer advanced study to prepare music scholars will be limited to those institutions having the outstanding scholarly resources on their faculties, and in their libraries, essential to the preparation of scholars and researchers in historical and theoretical musicology. The gamut of institutions for advanced study will be completed by a few institutions with exemplary resources for pursuing research and developing scholarships in the teaching of music and the areas of knowledge pertinent to it such as the psychology of music, the sociology of music, curriculum development, and evaluation of musical learning.

Major institutions will develop the resources for performance and research-oriented programs focused on popular and ethnic musics and jazz. The Benny Goodmans and Billie Holidays of the future will find productive places in those institutions both as students and faculty members.

Other institutions will adopt roles in musical education consistent with their resources and the needs of their clienteles. Undergraduate programs in one, two, or all three of the traditions in musical education will be appropriate for some institutions with comprehensive resources of high quality; fewer institutions will offer master's degree programs and only a few with stellar resources will offer doctoral programs in any field of musical education.

Music departments with limited resources will recognize the futility of offering *any* major in music, and will put their resources to work on an essential role—the musical education of the general college student. Furthermore, all but a few specialized institutions will place greater emphasis on offering courses and other experiences designed for and attractive to the general college student. The audiences and amateur musicians developed in such programs will strengthen the fabric of the musical culture.

Many music departments will provide expanded programs for elementary teachers in preparation designed to develop essential musical and pedagogical skills required in the elementary school music program. Music departments in institutions with strong programs in leisure studies will develop programs providing preparation in music for persons preparing to work in recreation and leisure programs administered by public agencies other than the public schools.

The Benefits of Change

What difference will the suggested changes in musical education make? What benefits will accrue? I suggest the following:

1. The music faculties of collegiate institutions and public schools will at long last accept the premise that music is a unified but varied art with a remote and a recent past and a present; an art with a variety of styles and genres, each of which functions in its unique way to express and ennoble the spirit of mankind.

2. Public school, college, and private music teachers will be involved in a broad enterprise of musical education characterized by cooperation and mutual support with the result that the quality of music students entering collegiate institutions and the quality of music teachers will be improved. Furthermore, the worth of the musical education gained by the general student will be enhanced.

3. The music establishment and the public will come to view the art of music as a diverse but unified cultural resource whose many styles are available both to the common man and to the elite in the society. Every man and woman will be able to control the aesthetic quality of his or her life, and will have a basis for making aesthetic choices.

4. Programs of musical education at every level will encompass the entire gamut of music, including the best of the old and the new among serious music, folk music, popular music, and jazz. The compositions of contemporary American composers will receive the hearing they require and merit.

5. Each college music department will be enabled to adopt and pursue a role in musical education consistent with its resources and the needs of its clientele. As a result, the overall quality of musical education will be enhanced. The most talented young musicians will have the advantage of the best musical education the country has to offer; those with lesser talent will not develop unrealistic expectations; they will, on the other hand, pursue a musical education and find a role in the musical establishment consistent with their abilities. The general student will have access to a richer program of music study and performance. The role of the amateur musician will receive increased impetus.

6. Major collegiate institutions will develop programs for the preparation of music administrators utilizing resources in the colleges of commerce and business administration, colleges of education, and schools and departments of music. The programs will include professional courses and an internship experience and will lead to a degree or other certification comparable to the M.B.A.

7. Changes in the public school music program seem inevitable, but with proper direction, the quality and achievement of the program can be enhanced rather than damaged. In the elementary school, I propose a return to a simple affordable music program which emphasizes teaching all children to sing and to play classroom and folk instruments; a program which builds a repertory of songs from the great European and American folk traditions, and from the best contemporary folk and popular music. It is essential that all children be initiated into instrumental experience both to give them functional skills with the notation and with folk instruments, and to whet their interest for traditional instruments.

The elementary school music program must permit and encourage the participation of elementary classroom teachers in music instruction. A concomitant is that two types of music personnel be prepared to assist and work with elementary classroom teachers: elementary teachers with a good solid minor in music and skilled specialist music consultants. A program directed by music consultants and taught by elementary classroom teachers can result in concrete achievement in musical literacy and in performance skills which students can use outside the classroom.

In the middle school and junior high school, a performance-oriented program of general music, choral music, and instrumental music is essential with listening and composition integral parts of all three types of classes.

We will maintain a strong corps of instrumental specialists able to teach both wind and string instruments and to work at all three levels of the public school.

The shape of the high school program will probably change in several respects. While large performance groups, including the marching band, will remain viable activities, they will, in many schools, be scheduled for fewer than five days each week, and will not claim the interest of many students throughout their school careers due to expanded curricular requirements mandated by state legislatures and demanded by college entrance officials. An expanded program of small ensembles will offer performance outlets for students unable to participate in large performance groups and excellent experience for aspiring musicians and music teachers.

The developing scholastic climate affords music educators the opportunity and the obligation to develop a solid course in the structure and styles of music at the high school level, a course which will satisfy the demands of college entrance officials for substantive content. It will be a course in fine arts that qualifies for inclusion in college entrance requirements.

8. A combination of factors: a) the decrease in school age population, b) the increase in the population beyond school age, and c) the growing difficulty of many public schools in financing a music program, means that the clientele for the school music program must be broadened to include young adults, people of middle age, and senior citizens. This must be accompanied by a comparable broadening of the base of financial support to include not only school districts, but also city, township, and country governments, arts councils, park districts,

and recreation commissions, in cooperative sponsorship of a comprehensive music program designed to appeal to the musical interests and aspirations of the total population of the community.

Such a program will encompass performance activities including band, chorus and orchestra, small ensembles, folk singing groups, beginning class instruction for people of all ages in a variety of instruments including piano, guitar, recorder, and the traditional band and orchestra instruments, opportunities for organized and informal listening experience and for composing music.

The program will be funded by tax monies from the school district and other participating government agencies. Facilities for the program would include school buildings, community centers, arts centers, senior citizens centers, and other available buildings.

Teachers may work in both school and community programs, either with joint appointments between the school and a community agency, or with a school district appointment partially funded by monies from one or more governmental agencies. The total program of school and community music will be coordinated and administered by a director of music education with joint-agency responsibility and authority. We will have a new generation of Mabelle Glenns and Russell Morgans.

9. Finally, we must seek to establish a broad coalition of professional and amateur musicians and other arts practitioners, arts educators in public and private schools, private teachers of music, and individuals and organizations concerned with the arts and arts education, to participate in political and social action at the local, state, and federal levels of government. A Common Cause for the Arts, if you will.

Coda

Now let us recapitulate a theme that has undergirded this seminar. Music exists to enrich the sentient life of our people. Musical Education exists to enable all of our people, rich and poor, young and old, to control the aesthetic quality of their lives and to make that aesthetic quality a matter of choice, not a matter of chance. We are in the business of Aesthetic Education, which has as its mission the development of the human capacity for thoughtful feeling and feelingful thought.

I believe that Howard Hanson, whom we celebrate this week, would have approved of this program of change. He did participate in the total music enterprise of the United States, and had a productive relationship with the school music program. His concerns ranged from the musical education of the common man to that of the artist performer and composer. He was concerned, and he had a beneficent influence not only on the collegiate programs of musical education, but also on the public school program and on continuing education in music for lay persons. It is appropriate that I close by quoting with reverence his charge to the Music Supervisors National Conference in 1932. It pertains as cogently in 1983 as it did more than fifty years ago. He said: "We are at last embarked on the search for national self-expressions through music. It is a golden road and one which in these days of spiritual poverty promises rich rewards. It is only for us who carry the torch to realize our responsibilities to see to it that the path to a glorious belief in the appreciation of beauty is cleared of its obstacles." I shall only add, Hanson's challenge was and is great; the rewards can be magnificent.

Summary of Group Discussions

The discussion groups focused on four main topics of Leonhard's presentation: music teacher preparation at the collegiate level, the use of popular, folk, and ethnic music in the public music classroom, the role of the music educator within the community and the nation, and the place of general music in the public school music curriculum.

There was general agreement that there must be a change in preparing music educators at the collegiate level. It was felt that many music educators are inadequately trained. This obviously leads to inferior music programs in the public schools. A suggestion was made to review the use of permanent teacher certification; this was thought to lead to some stagnation among teachers.

There was disagreement over Leonhard's idea of confining musical education institutions to certain types of musical training: conservatory, teaching, or research. Many group members opposed this idea because they felt college freshmen had not yet had the time to solidify their goals and career plans. The idea of reserving a few institutions for training the gifted and outstanding performers was an elitist idea in itself and did not consider late developing musicians. Group members reacted favorably to Leonhard's suggested curriculum reforms. Some felt that the programs were not very practical to implement.

There was consensus regarding a lack of communication between many university music education departments and public school music programs. Philosophy has been left at the collegiate level and practical application has been left to the public schools. More field teaching experiences were suggested for undergraduate music education majors. This would serve as practical experience for the student early in the college program while helping bridge a communication gap between the university and the public school.

There was strong agreement regarding the use of more popular and folk music. It was suggested that these materials should be drawn from many cultures. Emphasis should be put on how music is utilized in different cultures: The use of popular and folk styles may help to reach more public school students.

The diminishing role of general music skills in the public schools was mentioned. It was stated by one participant that general music sets the tone and atmosphere for the entire music program. He went on to say that it is probably the most important single part of the program and is the most difficult to teach. It was mentioned that there should be less emphasis on performance in the public schools and more emphasis on general music skills. We must inspire more students to teach general music rather than to become band or choral directors.

Great importance was placed on the role of the music educator in the community and the nation. Today's music educators must be aware of their role in the community. They must understand the political aspects and issues facing them in the task of development of political stategies as a high priority item.

Participants agreed that change is inevitable if music education is to survive. Leonhard's speech was important because it identified some of our serious problems, and identification is a major step toward solving them.

On the Need for
Bridging Music's Islands

ROBERT FREEMAN

A preliminary acquaintance with music in America during the 1980s indicates that there is much we can be proud of. Our high school band, orchestra, and chorus programs produce young musicians of promise who apply in great numbers to more than 500 schools and departments accredited by the National Association of Schools of Music. Our collegiate schools and departments develop performers for professional orchestras and opera houses, spread all over America, that are second to none in Europe or elsewhere. Our National Endowment for the Arts, now more than fifteen years old, has even in days of federal cutbacks attained a funding level that Americans in the day of John F. Kennedy would not have dreamed. Performing arts centers have been developed in communities both large and small all over the country. Chamber Music America has assisted in the recent development of what many see as a national chamber music boom. The Public Broadcasting System, National Public Radio, and a host of cable networks now make good music accessible in areas where it had never been previously. Private record libraries and those in major colleges and universities now make a breadth of musical literature available which would have been inconceivable at the time we were children.

But in the midst of these apparently favorable indications, there exists a broad array of serious problems. The nation's educational enterprise, beset with problems of finance, declining enrollments, and insufficient common purpose, has tended during the past several years to cut back on curricula not perceived as "basic." Our colleges and universities, troubled by continuing inflation, the threat of declining enrollments, and of federal cutbacks in the availability of student scholarship and loan funds, look warily ahead to a period in which it is predicted that a great many institutions will founder or merge. The National Endowment and state arts councils are themselves subject to a period of much slower financial growth, thus losing an important aspect of their ability to protect professional performing arts groups from the forays of inflation. The recording of "serious" music, once possible as part of the profit margin provided by "pop" recordings, stagnates in a period of retrenchment, the apparent victim of video games and unchecked home copying. The professional performing organizations, labor intensive as they are, all complain about broadening budget gaps which threaten program. PBS and NPR have themselves a budget deficit for the present year of something more than $7 million, a gap which they are trying to fill through contributions from member stations, themselves in financial peril.

A southern senator whose candidacy for the Presidency was announced two or three months ago once told me at lunch that his constituents accord "serious" music about as high a priority as they give to prison reform. But if Americans grant the performing arts a relatively low priority in an age troubled by our concerns for national productivity, for the future of our environment, for equal opportunities for the races, for national defense, and for a high level of national un-employment, we should not despair. Our nation, just having passed its two hun-dredth birthday, is still relatively young. Our Puritan origins, our strongly mer-cantile roots, and the comparatively recent closing of the American frontier all help explain why the performing arts in America have remained till now the con-cern of a relatively small number of people, some of whom pursue their interests in music, drama, and dance, for example, partly as a badge of aristocracy in a republic that has long stressed the importance of more populist traditions.

A useful example of the kind of thing I have in mind may be drawn from events that followed the tragic fire of the principal performance facilities at Wolf Trap. Washington society and a host of well-motivated performing artists sprang into action in an effort privately to raise funds needed for reconstruction. As the result of a good deal of effort a small part of the large sum needed for re-construction was in fact raised. That the reconstruction commenced despite so small a nest egg is easily explained by the fact that Wolf Trap is part of the Na-tional Parks System. Thus, so far as I understand things, the reconstruction of Wolf Trap was in fact a federal obligation, as much so as would be the hypo-thetical reconstruction, say, of principal public facilities at Yellowstone Na-tional Park. That an important show of private fund raising was undertaken in the case of Wolf Trap stems not from any fiscal necessity but rather, I believe, from a political sensitivity to the allocation of public funds for a purpose general-ly perceived to be elitist. Indeed, at a dinner in New York City to which I was in-vited several years ago a well-known society leader in that city expressed concern for what she thought my misconception that the performing arts in America will require a broader base of public support in the years ahead. Said she, "Mr. Freeman, you speak as though the arts belonged to all Americans, while in fact, a relatively small number of us have repeatedly provided the financial support that makes the arts possible. In my view, the arts belong to me and to my friends."

This paper has two theses. The first is that, in the years ahead, music in America will need broad support from both public and private sectors. As the result, we shall need the continuing generosity of the lady just quoted, and of her friends! We shall also need a clearer sense on the part of a broader number of Americans that music of the kind discussed these past several days will be vital to the country as a whole. The second thesis of my paper develops the notion that modern musical institutions in the United States may be construed as a series of islands, an archipelago, if you will. While I do not argue the need for anything like a national music policy, I am troubled by the idea that the natives of each of the several islands are accustomed to proceed without much knowledge of or in-terest in the activities of those on any of the other islands. In what follows I shall try, in no particular order, to describe the outlooks of several tribes of natives.

Though it is always risky to generalize about a nation whose educational as-pirations and attainments are so pluralistic as those in America, I think it safe to say that music in the public schools is normally set up so that "general music" is taught in the K-6 curriculum by music specialists who visit classrooms in the sys-tems where they are employed for thirty or sixty minutes per week. Because music is so little understood by the normal classroom teachers responsible for the curricula in those grades, there is a regrettable tendency for the music specialists to be treated by both classroom teacher and students as though music activities were more closely related to recess than to the work of the day.

During the grades 7-12 more and more attention is devoted to the performance activities of an increasingly select group of students whose bands, orchestras, and choruses take part in a seemingly endless round of local, regional, state, and national competitions. Surely these activities produce much that is positive. Large ensemble performance helps develop a greater sense of teamwork, useful to society generally. The local existence of a prizewinning ensemble acts positively towards the development of community pride. Such curricula are extremely helpful in the development of high school seniors who have applied during the past decade in growing numbers each year to professional schools like Eastman. There is no doubt but that such programs help sell large numbers of clarinets, band uniforms, metronomes, practice rooms, and cakes of resin. But I know of no study suggesting that those who win first prize in the all-state competitions show any greater interest in music after their graduation from high school than does the population generally. (I would count as "interest in music" any continuing interest in performance on the professional or amateur level, or any propensity to support music as a listener, through the purchase of records or of tickets to live concerts.)

Surely, music is an important spiritual and aesthetic force, as Howard Hanson said, so often and with such force. But the natives of the K-12 island will remain cut off from the broader aspects of our musical culture so long as they fail to follow through on the longer-term implications of their curricula for the musical lives and interests of high school graduates in the years that follow adolescence.

Meanwhile, the professional schools bravely graduate 20,000 people each year, a great many of whom dream of careers on the stage. At Eastman we pride ourselves on the honesty with which our catalogue treats the problem in "serious" music of oversupply for a lagging demand. But the deans of too many collegiate schools of music believe that any effort to introduce students to the realities of the professional world undermines a student's self-confidence, and is something akin to playing God. It is my own strong conviction that, in the years ahead, music will need all of the help we can give her. To my way of thinking, that means the development of musicians who are dedicated at least as much to the future of music as they are to the unfolding of their own careers. Certainly, it means the continuing development of young players and singers able to perform on the highest possible artistic level. But it also implies, I think, musicians familiar with the musical literature, well versed in music history and theory, and equipped to speak and write suasively and with enthusiasm about music and about music coherence. Such professionals, we hope, will remember the importance of nurturing throughout their careers the love of music which brought them here in the first place.

I am sorry to say, however, that in many an institution continuing emphasis on unnecessarily long days of practice, in preparation for competitions from which there will be many more losers than winners, produces jaded musicians who view teaching, or performance in a major orchestra, as a kind of personal defeat. Like the inhabitants of the K-12 island, those who teach and study in the professional schools would be well advised to remember that most of the students will have to graduate, and that the other islands of the archipelago are not well served by those who believe that their destiny should be limited to the stage of the Metropolitan Opera or to the principal oboe chair in the Boston Symphony Orchestra.

Two or three dozen of the 20,000 people who graduate each year from America's professional music schools will win first prize in an important national or international competition. Those competing will realize, by the time they finish the competitions, if they do not realize at the beginning, that the judging of such contests reflects the tastes of the jurors, and is thus, inevitably, both political and arbitrary. It has always seemed to me as a sometime juror myself that my own chance of predicting the winner of a performance competition is not better than one in the number of contestants, divided by two. The probabilities of my picking the winner seems similar to me to the probability that I will pick the winner of the annually televised Miss America Pageant. Though I have not kept records on the subject, my reminiscence strongly sugggests that in the years when I pick Miss Arizona, it is always Miss New Hampshire who wins. Thus, when I admire the Chopin playing of the young Pole, it is always the Rachmaninov playing of the young Russian which carries the day.

However destructive and arbitrary such competitions may seem to young performers and to those who teach them, the inhabitants of the island whose geographic center is West 57th Street, New York City, believe that they serve the national interest. I was told three months ago by the president of one of that island's largest management firms that the trouble with music school directors is that they believe the sky is falling. "Why," said the president, "there are two hundred virtuosi in the country today each of whom earns more than $250,000 a year." As chief of that island, the president's concern for the musical life of the country as a whole is satisfied by the fact that his firm collects 20 percent of the fees of at least half of those virtuosi. An unhappy aspect of the philosophy promulgated by the island on 57th Street concerns the repertory required for the competitions. Because this is necessarily narrow, students who seek to win such competitions are obliged to see to it that their training is narrow. In the hope of a slightly more polished performance of the Tchaikovsky B-flat concerto a young pianist will feel obliged to ignore the chamber music of Brahms, the songs of Schubert, and anything written since the death of Webern. Thus, while the present competition system well serves the needs of the 57th Street island, the public relations mentality that it fosters does not help the needs of the composers, of the smaller communities in the country, or even of the larger orchestras.

Since most of the concertgoing public knows about music only what it reads in the newspaper, it believes itself poorly served unless it hears what is proclaimed by some Pope of taste to be the very best. No orchestra in the country can break even on the $55,000 asking price of the best known violinist in the land, but the man in question fills not only the house, but helps sell the series as well. What is one to say if the public which demands the $55,000 artist by voting with its feet could not discern the aural difference between that very distinguished man and another excellent player whose asking price is less than a tenth as much? How are young musicians to interpret this syndrome, and what does it do to the development of their priorities?

Three Thousand Futures, a recent publication of the Carnegie Commission on Education which tries to develop strategies for the survival of at least the majority of this country's colleges and universities, puts forward a number of arguments why Americans in the years ahead should continue to wish to go to college. Among the arguments there adduced are claims that a college education will increase one's income, improve one's tolerance of religious and political diversity, encourage one's investment in common stocks, and improve a person's interpersonal relationship with his or her spouse and children. In all of these areas a college education is said to improve probabilities by factors ranging from .15 to .95. In the whole argumentation of the Carnegie Commission there is but one parameter in which a college education increases probabilities by a factor of more than 1: the likelihood that an adult will seek to attend performances of "serious" music. That the fact of college attendance in a society so pluralistic as ours increases this probability by a factor of more than 3 if one is male, and by more than 4 if one is female, should give us all pause. Still, on the island inhabited by America's university professors of music, tenure is awarded on the basis of scholarly and compositional productivity, seldom as the result of one's ability to draw larger numbers of enthusiastic students into introductory music courses. As the recent CMS Conference at Wingspread has shown, introductory college courses in music, certainly the most difficult to teach, are normally assigned to those most junior in rank and lowest in salary.

While thinking a moment about the collegiate island, it seems appropriate to pause on the role of composers. There was a day in the history of music when the patrons decided which kinds of music they wished to hear more of. Following the French Revolution these patrons tended to disappear from the scene, thus leading to Hans Sachs' remark in the first act of *Die Meistersinger von Nürnberg*, "so lasst das Volk auch Richter sein" ("In judging matters of art it is appropriate to let the people be the judge"). But in the modern American university, the principal support of the "serious" American composer, neither the *cognoscenti* nor the people are allowed to judge, but rather the composers themselves. This insular tendency may be good for academic governance, but I do not believe that it well serves the broader interests of music.

Rowing carefully over the shoals to the island of music journalism, it is easy for us to understand the managing editor who requires that his music critic write English with flair, have a solid, journalistic background to write feature stories, and know something about music. Unfortunately, too many managing editors notice that the crowds for the National Football League or for the Rolling Stones are larger than those for symphonic or chamber music. They infer as a result that since their newspapers represent a business, there is very little point in employing a full-time music critic to address so relatively small a portion of their reading public. Music criticism, they reason, sells few newspapers. As a result, they tend to hire music critics not from the outside but from existing staff, and here the requirement that the person hired "know something about music" gets us all into a lot of trouble. The managing editor does not require that the critic have ears. And the fact that a critic on a smaller paper can get himself promoted to a larger paper, and a bigger salary, by writing aggressively is of no concern to the touring virtuosi. They, after all, simply cull the lines they need for their press brochures from the contexts in which they occur. But the aggressive critic may have a compellingly negative effect on the future of local institutions. Both the seat-buying public and the governing board normally know even less about music than the critic, and especially in matters of the arts people tend to accept what they read in the newspaper as though it were the truth rather than a matter of opinion. In this context the development of a new program for the education of music critics at the Peabody Conservatory of Johns Hopkins University is much to be applauded.

The rather large island represented by the American Symphony Orchestra League has expanded markedly during the past fifteen years, the result, it is said, of the generous Ford Foundation program of the late 1960s and of the increasingly important role in the meantime of the National Endowment for the Arts and of the state arts councils. Highly labor intensive, even the orchestras which fill all their seats are caught in an economic vise driven on the one hand by inflation and the resulting need to pay higher salaries, and on the other by their apparent inability to raise ticket prices in anything like a manner to keep pace. One of the results is a tendency to perform more concerts and to rehearse less. Another result is the increased tendency to concentrate on standard repertory at the expense of the unfamiliar, especially of the new.

Symptomatic in this connection is the public's, and the papers', insistence that the world of "new" music began with the death of Brahms, before, that is, the birth of those of us who are now ninety years old. There was a day on the orchestral island, not so long ago, when music directors took an active role in the development not only of the personnel of their orchestra but in the musical life of their orchestra's community. The jet plane has changed all that. Conductors, as human as the rest of us after all, perceive that it is both easier and more lucrative to conduct a dozen new pieces each year all over the world than to stay home and to learn one hundred new pieces.

It has been argued of late on the orchestral island that something must be done about the inadequate training provided in American music schools for American conductors. There is, to be sure, a continuing problem in music schools on both sides of the Atlantic affecting the training of conductors: the teachers of string players, always in short supply, take an understandably negative view of dedicating much of their students' valuable time to orchestral performance under student conductors. It has always seemed to me, as the director of a major music school, that the problem comes rather from young Americans'

perception that the boards of the largest American orchestras find a music director from abroad of exotic appeal to potential concertgoers. At a time when the
music director of the Vienna State Opera is an American, there is something
deeply ironic, I agree with Irving Kolodin, about a situation in which the music
directors of the six American orchestras with the largest budgets come from
Japan, India, Italy, Hungary, and Germany, respectively.

Many of the orchestras have come to realize that the rotation of string seating can be a powerful antidote to the poison of routine that accompanies sitting
for many years at a stretch sixty feet or more from the ears (and the attention) of
the conductor. Still, orchestral committees and the musicians' union tend still to
frustrate the possibility of a broader musical life made possible by teaching, solo,
and chamber playing. Such people tend to ignore the deadening effect of routine
on practice and artistic aspiration that comes from years of *tutti* playing in a
choir where one's individuality as a musician is submerged.

Among the most insular of the phenomena, even in a world of small islands,
are the educational programs of the American orchestras. These seem to operate
in isolation from the artistic leadership of the orchestras, from those responsible
for the development of program booklets, and from the part of the collegiate
world that dedicates its attention to introductory courses in music.

The world of recording made a vast contribution to musical literacy during
the 1950s and 1960s, following the invention of the long-playing record. But although not every work has been recorded which should be, there is a growing
sense in the industry that it is not so much the recording of unfamiliar literature
from the past or present which will sell, but the re-recording of already familiar
repertory with new artists or with new technology. Partly because of economic
pressures affecting the "pop" world and because of recent restrictions on credit,
the means of distribution for "serious" recordings have become much more
limited than before. As a result a much smaller repertory is available on the
shelves of those record stores that survive, and the person seriously interested is
obliged to do much of his business by mail order or by home taping. The narrow
bridge to the mainland which used to exist is in bad repair, often washed out by
high tides.

The development of concert music radio stations following World War II
promised at one time, I think, to become an important bridge-building force in
the world of music, along the lines perhaps of the BBC's Third Program. But the
relatively small and local nature of the public for good music in America has
placed economic constraints on the growth of such an enterprise. Many of the
good music stations have failed to survive; now some of those that have devote a
substantial part of their daily programming to public affairs. Anyone who drives
across the United States will remark on the vast preponderance of stations carrying other repertories, a monopolistic business whose proprietors, as Gunther
Schuller has correctly pointed out, have no interest in helping promulgate any
repertory whose profit margin is smaller.

Foundation aid for the performing arts has been until the very recent past a
disappointingly occasional matter and one often restricted to the support of local

institutions. The music program of the National Endowment for the Arts, before Frank Hodsoll's leadership, proclaimed that its only role in the distribution of naturally finite resources would have to be the preservation of existing professional institutions. Much credit is to be given to Mr. Hodsoll and his people for the realization that the Endowment's role as a potential bridge builder could stimulate corporate foundations into similar activity. Hodsoll's realization that the kinds of professional artists now being educated in the 1980s will inevitably affect the quality of America's cultural life during the twenty-first century has brought about his attendance at and participation in this conference, a point which I hope will prove to be of special significance for the future as the result of NEA advocacy for educational reform.

Because time this afternoon is short, I have not tried to catalogue all of the islands in music's archipelago. I hope, nonetheless, that by cataloguing at least some of the principal islands and their isolation from one another I have been able to sketch a significant part of our problem. Improved means of communication among the islands are needed. To accomplish this we should develop, I believe, more comprehensively trained and educated musicians, young men and women better motivated to help expand music's role in American society. Helpful, too, would be the development of strategies designed to expose larger numbers of Americans to good music. I do not dream of a day in which all those who go to baseball games listen doggedly to string quartets. If we could reach a situation in which even half of the country's college graduates were avocationally dedicated to good music, we would have made great progress.

At present most Americans think of music of the kind under discussion here as belonging to someone else. Audience studies on our annual "Prism" concerts here at Eastman indicate that those attending a concert of music from the 1920s in order to hear the Gershwin and Porter often find that the works by Bartok and Stravinsky which they expected *not* to like were attractive enough to impel attendance at concerts featuring such repertory. The problem, I believe, is exposure, and at as early an age as possible. Kenneth Wendrich is now urging the importance of musical day care centers fostering aural perception in infants and preschool children. Jeanne Bamberger has developed a variety of strategies that make musical perception potentially an important part of cognitive development for those in an elementary school environment. The recent report on the President's Commission for Educational Excellence, "A Nation at Risk," outlines education's problems in our society generally, and calls for broad-reaching reform.

Certainly, music is aesthetic; that we assembled at this Conference are all musicians results primarily from our common dedication to music. But it has always seemed to me that our role in persuading the rest of society of music's aesthetic quality is not unlike that of a group of French actors anxious to perform on a regular basis the classics of French tragic theater in Berlin. Several of us are gifted in telling the Berliners of the great aesthetic beauty of French tragedy, well performed. But our audiences are normally quite small, for there are after all in Berlin relatively few people who understand French. Carrying the same metaphor a bit further, we music teachers must recognize, I believe, that too often we teach students to speak French, as it were, who have no idea of what they are saying.

When educational reformers stress the importance of what they normally call the basics, reading and writing, I try to remind them that what is really basic is thought—that reading and writing are in fact only the agents of synthesis and cogent analysis. Threatened as we are by a society whose political judgments are increasingly the result of suasion by televised slogans, we should seek out educational means which will increase cognitive capacity. If listening to music that is not simplistic from an early age helps develop cognitive capacity, I would argue that aural memory should be encouraged from an early age, and as a central part of our K-12 curricula. A national radio network making broader repertories available to larger numbers of Americans would, I believe, also be extremely helpful.

It may turn out in the end that tunnels and bridges among the islands are simply too expensive a public works enterprise to undertake at this time in our national history. I hope I have demonstrated the need at least for some regularly scheduled ferries, and a telephone or two.

Question and Answer Session

QUESTION: Where do you see specific leadership coming from in the building of bridges—tunnels or airways—that you have alluded to?

FREEMAN: From each of us, really. I think it would be a mistake for me to say that leaders in all of this have to be either in Group A, B, or C. The people who are teachers and administrators of major professional music schools have an important responsibility to look to the breadth of the educational commitment that they are developing in the musicians and teachers of the future. I also believe that those of us who are engaged in daily classroom activities have a tremendously important responsibility as well.

QUESTION: What kind of suggestions can you give to help establish greater unity?

FREEMAN: I think it's up to each of us to do his or her best, to take a larger view of what the possibilities are. As musicians—composers, theorists, musicologists, pianists, oboists, conductors—we have not thought very much about how to address people who don't have any notion about why the first two measures of the Beethoven Eighth Symphony lead to the third and fourth measures. People would like to be given some help on what to do, but when we talk about musical instruction, far too often the subject is how to perform the first four measures of the Eighth Symphony: "I'll play for you three common mistakes, and then you're going to imitate whatever I'm telling you about ways to correct that." We are not concerned enough about opening people's minds and ears to what makes a piece of music cohere. If, for example, you want to talk to fifteen-year-old kids about Ravel's *Bolero* (as a result of having seen Bo Derek in "Ten"), they have some idea of what the piece is like. The kind of thing I have in mind saying is, "Look, the Ravel *Bolero* involves a very simple repeated rhythmic pattern. It's invariant throughout the whole piece. And the piece is based on equally simple harmonic patterns.

[At this point Dr. Freeman illustrates by performing at the piano while continuing his comments.] The conductor has to begin very softly and he has to hold the piece in a steady tempo while letting the dynamic range gradually increase. If he allows the dynamic range to increase too soon the piece is dead. Some of the players are going to have difficulty playing some of the rather difficult solos. The piece also involves a series of repetitions of "A," and something similar that can be called "B." You get AABB four times. Finally, you get AB without any repeats. That, and the fact that the piece has gotten as loud as it possibly can get—at least if you haven't heard some recent rock and roll manifestations—will persuade you that the work is about to conclude.

What I just said isn't very complicated. But it gives an intelligent person who has never heard that piece before something to do while listening to it unfold. It may even give some people who are professional musicians playing in the orchestra something to do. [laughter]

I'm not throwing rocks at the public. I'm saying that we as musicians have not been accustomed in the course of the history of music to think of ways of explicating the unfolding of a piece which are both faithful to the music and at the same time of interest to people of normal intelligence.

QUESTION: We've heard a great deal of presentation in our various speeches as to an analysis of where we are and where we should be going. I wonder if you see any way that we can have a common cause, a strategy, or a plan to implement some of these ideas, and to move into a "phase two" of this conference. One in which we would be concerned with how it might be carried into action.

FREEMAN: I don't want to appear as though I think that I know what prescription is best for music in the United States. Forgive me for even trying to answer your question. But you asked it, and I'm standing on the stage.

The first thing I would ask you all to remember every day of your lives is the reason we are all musicians: We love music. There was something about the combination of tones which we all found stirring, whether at the age of ten, or fifteen, or twenty. Listening to a Schubert song, listening to a piece of chamber music by Brahms, to a Monteverdi madrigal, or to an orchestra work by Stravinsky was in some sense exciting to each of us.

We wanted to be able to partake of the experience of composing music, or performing it, or bringing others to feel as deeply moved as we were in those days. Over time, one sometimes loses that joy in music. I'm always trying to remind young people at Eastman that at the time one loses that joy in music it's a good time to consider the possibility of employment in another field.

Second, as was indicated earlier, is that if this conference has meant something positive to you, you should seek to communicate that aspect of your excitement to your colleagues back home.

Third is that we shall certainly continue at Eastman in subsequent summers with an effort to develop the kind of curriculum which will move toward instruction in musical coherence. Please be aware that I'm not saying that the musicologists or the theorists have the answer. I'm deeply concerned, as a musicologist myself, by the fact that musicology has gone down a road in the last thirty years which tends to stress external, at the expense of internal, evidence. External evidence consists of factors like water marks and paper chemical analysis, which help to get the history of music straight; that's a worthwhile intellectual activity. But to the degree that in getting chronology and authenticity straight we lose enthusiasm about how to make a good case for the Ravel *Bolero*, for example, or for the last movement of the Beethoven Ninth, or for the second movement of the Brahms B Flat Sextet, that's regrettable.

One of the things we are trying at Eastman soon will be to stop school for a day or so—no classes, no lectures, no lessons—and to meet in this room with perhaps four or five faculty colleagues on stage or in the front row to discuss three or four pieces. Take a Schubert impromptu, or a Bach fugue, or a Beethoven minuet, and make the best case for the piece you can by playing it as beautifully as you can. *Then* be willing to accept the comments and criticisms of your colleagues who, as composers, teachers, theorists, musicologists, have different relationships to the piece—to see what other ways there are to perform the piece, to make it even more stunning.

Too often performers have the idea that there is "a way" to play the piece, and that the notes are all on the score once the musicologists have developed a critical text. Such people think that the music is all there and that all you have to do is "do it." Music making, however, takes a lot of imagination, and a lot of artistic sensitivity beyond what a critical text can provide. The critical text provides only the basis from which one can proceed.

QUESTION: Bob, I was really intrigued by Dr. Leonhard's suggestion of creating a series of Howard Cosells of music. After all, this summer you were running an institute for the training of sports organists. Why not a school for musical Howard Cosells?

FREEMAN: What do you mean by a musical Howard Cosell? [Question to Dr. Leonhard]

LEONHARD: Mr. Freeman and I were talking about a useful sports analogy. Color commentators have given the general public exactly the sort of information that connects things together and that you are suggesting is needed [in music] by many people. What I suggested this morning was that we should loosen up concerts so that instead of everything being so formal and solemn, we could have someone comment attractively. Maybe the conductor or somebody else could try to tell the audience what was in that piece and what he was going to do with it, so that gradually the audience would gain the ability to make discriminations about music—both in its performance and about its style—that are not only valid but important to them.

FREEMAN: I fully concur with the point you are making. Howard Cosell has been a great popularizer—though also sometimes a gadfly whom many sports fans don't like.

Let me talk about baseball—and baseball education—for a moment, with respect to music and music education. Kids learn baseball all over the United States from the age of four or five, when their mothers and fathers play ball with them in the backyard. They learn how to catch. They learn how to throw. They learn how to hit, in however primitive a fashion. They also do that in the schools, after church, and in the Little League. They learn fundamental baseball skills, but beyond that they learn something which I have always called the tactics and strategy of baseball. They learn what makes baseball, as a game, cohere. They learn that if you hit the ball you don't run to third base, you run to first base. To be sure, that's cognitive. You have to "know" to do that—in the same sense that Beethoven knew that before he could move on, he had to establish the initial tonal area of a piece. Anybody who knows baseball knows that if you succeed in getting to first base you look very carefully to see whether the next batter hits the ball on the ground, or in the air. If it's on the ground, you run right away, no matter what. If it's in the air, you hedge your bets.

What Howard Cosell and his colleagues do is to bring to the attention of the great sports-buying public the fact that baseball is a pretty interesting game. Now, I claim that there are a million different ways of watching a baseball game. My wife knows less baseball than I do, but she knows quite a lot. She enjoys watching the "Game of the Week" with me on Saturday—or at least she says she does.

I know less baseball than Billy Martin. I don't have scouting reports, I don't keep statistics, and I don't have any computer printouts on where to play my left-fielder. But I have a fair sense of the fact that Jim Rice of the Red Sox is a better fielder than he used to be and that I would be less willing than I would have been as a manager opposing the Red Sox in 1975 to let a runner of mine try to score on Jim Rice's arm. We all watch baseball in a variety of ways. Some people watch a baseball game with utter boredom. They go because somebody drags them to the game and they appreciate—if anything—the fact that the hot dog tasted good or that the grass is green. That's the experience I had in Cambridge, England, twelve years ago. I was working on some musicology Monday through Friday in the Fitzwilliam Museum. I took the train up on Sunday and looked out of my room to where two dozen people were playing cricket. For me, there had been no Howard Cosell for cricket. It looked like a lot of disorganized hitting, running, and throwing, and not much sliding—because they had very elegant long white pants.

The game went on for seven hours, and so far as I could tell it wasn't over when I finally gave up. It seems to me that most Americans, even in this concert hall, are in the position that I was in with respect to cricket, not in the position that I am with respect to baseball.

QUESTION: What are we going to do about providing this sort of commentary? Are we going to run an institute for the preparation of commentators sometime?

FREEMAN: I think we should all become commentators, each in his own sphere of activity. Anything in good taste for the repertory in question—in program notes or critical commentary from the stage, or commentary in radio programs—helps, if it is well done.

The commentator should provide a unifying element which opens one's ears to the music—a thread which makes the unfolding of the piece of music a more interesting experience.

QUESTION: You might be interested in an approach that was used in our city this past year. The local arts council sponsored a dinner which preceded a university production of "Man of La Mancha." It advertised that the musicologist at the university, Chappell White, would give educational information regarding the production. We expected a modest response. However, the place was filled with people. The university president decided that this would be a good time to invite the Board of Regents; all of them attended. They invited the Kansas Arts Commission. Every single state commissioner was there. There was not enough room. State legislators were there. It will be repeated. Chappell White did a beautiful job. The stage was set for beautiful public relations that evening.

FREEMAN: Thank you for letting us know that. That does indeed sound like something that could be replicated in other parts of the country.

Our job, as teachers who are trying to get the rest of the society in this young land of ours into music, should be to provide as many strategies as we can with respect to as many interesting and moving pieces as we can. That's the sort of thing I hope to continue with at Eastman beginning next summer.

Principal Speakers

Frank S. M. Hodsoll, Chairman, National Endowment for the Arts
  (Session chaired by Roy Ernst)
Christopher Lasch, Don Alonzo Watson Professor of History and Director of
  Graduate Studies in History, University of Rochester; author, *The Culture
  of Narcissism*
  (Session chaired by George Duerksen)
Russell P. Getz, President, Music Educators National Conference, and
  Associate Professor, Gettysburg College
  (Session chaired by Charles Fowler)
Sydney Hodkinson, Professor of Conducting and Ensembles, and Composi-
  tion, Eastman School of Music
  (Session chaired by Martin Mailman)
Willard L. Boyd, President, Field Museum of Natural History
  (Session chaired by Barbara English Maris)
Charles Leonhard, Professor of Music and Chairman of Graduate Studies in
  Music Education, University of Illinois; co-author, *Foundations and
  Principles in Music Education*
  (Session chaired by Will Schmid)
Robert Freeman, Director, Eastman School of Music
  (Session chaired by David Robinson)

Group Discussion Leaders

Jeanne Bamberger	Massachusetts Institute of Technology
George Duerksen	University of Kansas
Milford Fargo	Eastman School of Music
Charles Fowler	*Musical America*
Richard Grunow	Eastman School of Music
Barbara English Maris	Catholic University of America
Martin Mailman	North Texas State University
Jack Pinto	President, New York State School Music Association
David Robinson	Greece Central Schools
Will Schmid	University of Wisconsin-Milwaukee
Donald Shetler	Eastman School of Music
Kenneth Wendrich	Bowling Green State University

Conference Participants

Donna J. Autula	Eastman School of Music	Rochester, N.Y.
Jeanne Bamberger	Massachusetts Institute of Technology	Cambridge, Mass.
Richard R. Bentley	The Texas Woman's University	Denton, Tex.
Elizabeth Blades-Zeller	Eastman School of Music	Rochester, N.Y.
Zelman Bokser	Young Audiences, Inc.	Rochester, N.Y.
Roger Bookout	Monroe Community College	Rochester, N.Y.
Joseph Borrelli	Medina Central School District	Medina, N.Y.
Adele Bovard	Eastman School of Music	Rochester, N.Y.
Judith Bowman	Eastman School of Music	Rochester, N.Y.
Willard L. Boyd	Field Museum of Natural History	Chicago, Ill.
James M. Brinkman	Eastern Illinois University	Charleston, Ill.
Mary E. Brinkman	East Irondequoit School District	Rochester, N.Y.
Karon J. Cameron	First United Methodist Church	Gadsden, Ala.
Elaine F. Childs	University of Wyoming	Laramie, Wyo.
Gordon B. Childs	University of Wyoming	Laramie, Wyo.
Win Christian	New Mexico State Department of Education	Santa Fe, N.M.
Irene R. Christman	Pennsylvania Music Educators Association	Harrisburg, Pa.
Idonia Clark-Cannady	Eastman School of Music	Rochester, N.Y.
Ned Corman	Penfield Central Schools	Penfield, N.Y.
Kevin Coughlin	Rochester City School District	Rochester, N.Y.
Bill Covert	Portland Public Schools	Portland, Ore.
Mary Jane Crawford	Bennett College	Greensboro, N.C.
George Curfman	Lebanon Valley College	Annville, Pa.
Sandra Dackow	Slippery Rock State University of Pennsylvania	Slippery Rock, Pa.
Christine Warner Davis	Bradenton Christian School	Bradenton, Fla.
Karen Deans	*Music Educators Journal*	Reston, Va.
Edward A. DeDee	Eastman School of Music	Rochester, N.Y.
Christine DeLuca	Eastman School of Music	Rochester, N.Y.
Frank Dent	Young Audiences, Inc.	New York, N.Y.
George Duerksen	University of Kansas	Lawrence, Kans.
Margaret Dunlay		Rochester, N.Y.
Gerald A. Edgreen	Port Allegany High School	Port Allegany, Pa.
Charles A. Elliott	University of South Carolina	Columbia, S.C.
Jon Engberg	Eastman School of Music	Rochester, N.Y.
Judy Engberg		Rochester, N.Y.
Roy E. Ernst	Eastman School of Music	Rochester, N.Y.
Milford H. Fargo	Eastman School of Music	Rochester, N.Y.
Ernest R. Farmer	Summy-Birchard Music Co.	Princeton, N.J.
Colleen A. Foley	Brewster Academy	Wolfeboro, N.H.
Charles B. Fowler	*Musical America*	Washington, D.C.
Carrol Frangipane	Suzuki Piano Teacher Association	Rochester, N.Y.

Robert Freeman	Eastman School of Music	Rochester, N.Y.
Richard G. Gaarder	Wisconsin School Music Association, Inc.	Madison, Wis.
Linda Gerber	Western Connecticut State University	Woodbury, Conn.
Timothy Gerber	Susquehanna University	Selinsgrove, Pa.
Russell P. Getz	Gettysburg College and MENC President	Gettysburg, Pa.
Michele Gingras	Eastman School of Music	Rochester, N.Y.
Norman A. Goldberg	Magnamusic-Baton	St. Louis, Mo.
Robert Gray	Sir Sanford Fleming Secondary School	Toronto, Canada
Richard F. Grunow	Eastman School of Music	Rochester, N.Y.
Eloise Haldeman	Beverly Hills Unified School District	Los Angeles, Calif.
Edna L. Hansen	Port Clinton High School	Port Clinton, Ohio
Jack J. Heller	University of Connecticut	Storrs, Conn.
Ralph E. Hickman, Jr.	Eastman School of Music	Rochester, N.Y.
Sydney Hodkinson	Eastman School of Music	Rochester, N.Y.
Frank S. M. Hodsoll	National Endowment for the Arts	Washington, D.C.
Marguerite V. Hood	University of Michigan (retired)	Pomona, Calif.
Bryan C. Hunter	Nazareth College of Rochester	Rochester, N.Y.
Lawrence Huntley	Western Connecticut State University	Danbury, Conn.
Ridgely Hurt	Talladega County Schools	Sylacauga, Ala.
Ann Fabe Isaacs	National Association for Creative Children and Adults	Cincinnati, Ohio
Robert W. John	University of Georgia	Athens, Ga.
Carole J. Judd	State University College at Brockport	Brockport, N.Y.
Donald W. Justice	Eastman School of Music	Rochester, N.Y.
Susan H. Kenney	Brigham Young University	Sandy, Utah
Robert Lee Kidd, III	Eisenhower Elementary School	Norman, Okla.
Rosemary J. Koepfle	Ohio Music Education Association	Cincinnati, Ohio
Charles Krusenstjerna	Eastman School of Music	Rochester, N.Y.
Milford E. Kuhn, Jr.	Morehead State University	Morehead, Ky.
Allen Lanham	Inter-American University of Puerto Rico	San Germán, P.R.
Christopher Lasch	University of Rochester	Rochester, N.Y.
Sang-Hie Lee	University of Alabama	University, Ala.
Charles Leonhard	University of Illinois	Urbana, Ill.
Marvin W. Lewis	Port Jefferson Schools	Port Jefferson, N.Y.
Betty J. Looney	Yamaha International Corp.	Buena Park, Calif.
Nancy C. Lutz	Marion Community Schools	Marion, Ind.
Carol Lyle	Ohio Music Education Association	New Concord, Ohio
Douglas Lyle	Muskingum College (retired)	New Concord, Ohio
Leslee B. Mabe	Webster Central Schools	Webster, N.Y.
Martin Mailman	North Texas State University	Denton, Tex.
Barbara English Maris	Catholic University of America	Washington, D.C.
Quentin G. Marty	Westminster Choir College	Princeton, N.J.
Richard McCrystal	Rush-Henrietta Central Schools	Henrietta, N.Y.
Raymond A. Mech	Indiana State University	Terre Haute, Ind.

Robert Mee	Upper Canada College	Toronto, Canada
Joan Meier	Princeton High School	Cincinnati, Ohio
Robert Meier		Cincinnati, Ohio
Robert Miller	University of Connecticut	Storrs, Conn.
Beth Nelson	Eastman School of Music	Rochester, N.Y.
Sue Neuen	Eastman School of Music	Rochester, N.Y.
Melinda M. Noel	Buffalo Academy for the Visual and Performing Arts	Buffalo, N.Y.
Dorothy Okamitsu	Department of Education, State of Hawaii	Honolulu, Hawaii
Jack (Giacomo M.) Oliva	Leonia Public Schools	Leonia, N.J.
Lori Osgood	Eastman School of Music	Rochester, N.Y.
Emma Garmendia Paesky	Catholic University of America	Washington, D.C.
John Palermo	Rockway Township Board of Education	Bloomsbury, N.J.
Marcia B. Parkes	Eastman School of Music	Rochester, N.Y.
Sesta Peekstok	Arts for Greater Rochester	Rochester, N.Y.
Susan E. Peters	Fulton Consolidated Schools	Oswego, N.Y.
Irving B. Phillips	Eastman School of Music	Rochester, N.Y.
Jack Pinto	New York State School Music Association	Endicott, N.Y.
Glenn Price	Eastman School of Music	Rochester, N.Y.
Roger Edwin Reichmuth	Murray State University	Murray, Ky.
Elizabeth M. Reno	Carnegie-Mellon University	Pittsburgh, Pa.
Charles H. Reynolds	Anchorage School District	Anchorage, Alas.
Ann F. Rhody	Greece Central Schools	Greece, N.Y.
David Robinson	Greece Central Schools	Greece, N.Y.
Monica Rogers	Lincolnwood Schools	Lincolnwood, Ill.
Will Schmid	University of Wisconsin	Milwaukee, Wis.
Edna A. Schroeer	Durham Academy	Durham, N.C.
Harry Semerjian	Fitchburg State College	Lunenburg, Mass.
Donald J. Shetler	Eastman School of Music	Rochester, N.Y.
Richard H. Snook	Greece Central Schools	Greece, N.Y.
Don Snowden		Foley, Ala.
Linda Stradley Staiger	Alfred-Almond Central School	Alfred Station, N.Y.
Paul Stencel	Daemen College	Amherst, N.Y.
Jack R. Stephenson	University of Missouri-Kansas City	Kansas City, Mo.
Mildred Stirzaker	McCracken Junior High School	Spartanburg, S.C.
Lee R. Suman	Ohio Music Education Association	Cincinnati, Ohio
Shirley R. Suman	Ohio Music Education Association	Cincinnati, Ohio
Robert M. Taras	Eastman School of Music	Rochester, N.Y.
Lois Taylor	Eastman School of Music	Rochester, N.Y.
Beverly Thornhill	Roy J. Maier Products	Sun Valley, Calif.
Mary R. Tolbert	Ohio State University	Columbus, Ohio
Laree M. Trollinger	Kutztown State University	Reading, Pa.
Valerie Vance	Young Audiences of Western New York	Buffalo, N.Y.
Loren R. Waa	University of Louisville	Louisville, Ky.

Bret Waller	Memorial Art Gallery	Rochester, N.Y.
Geraldine M. Ward	Westminster Choir College	Princeton, N.J.
Matthew J. Weber	McAllen High School	McAllen, Tex.
Linda B. Weis	Manhattan Middle School	Manhattan, Kans.
Paul N. Weise	Columbus College	Columbus, Calif.
Kenneth A. Wendrich	Bowling Green State University	Bowling Green, Ohio
Jeanette Wilhelm	Brighton Central Schools	Brighton, N.Y.
Larry D. Williams	Great Falls Public Schools	Great Falls, Mont.
Norman Woodall	Knoxville Central High School	Knoxville, Tenn.
Ellis C. Worthen	Granite School District Office	Salt Lake City, Utah
Irene Yang	Eastman School of Music	Rochester, N.Y.
Jeffrey D. Young	Buffalo High School	Buffalo, N.Y.
William T. Young	Stephen F. Austin State University	Nacogdoches, Tex.